DATE DUE

UNFINISHED BUSINESS

JAMES VAN PRAAGH

unfinished
BUSINESS

What the Dead Can Teach Us About Life

HarperOne
An Imprint of HarperCollinsPublishers

HarperOne

HarperCollins books may be purchased for educational, business, or sales promotional use. For information please write: Special Markets Department, Harper-Collins Publishers, 10 East 53rd Street, New York, NY 10022.

HarperCollins Web site: http://www.harpercollins.com

HarperCollins®, 📖®, and HarperOne™ are trademarks of HarperCollins Publishers

FIRST EDITION

Library of Congress Cataloging-in-Publication Data is available upon request.

ISBN 978–0–06–177814–8

09 10 11 12 13 RRD(H) 10 9 8 7 6 5 4 3 2 1

To Linda Tomchin
My earthly angel who assists me
in nurturing the minds
and opening the hearts of the masses.
For you, I am forever grateful.

CONTENTS

PROLOGUE

Ginny Meyer looked at her watch. The large hand closed in on the eleven while the small one touched the five. Neil would be coming home from work any second now, she thought. Ben wouldn't be alone for too long. Besides, Ben and his little friend Andrew were glued to the television set. Their eyes were probably glazed over as they watched the latest installment of the wildly successful Japanese cartoon *Pokémon*. For kids lost in the world of Pokémon, moms are just background noise. The boys didn't even notice Ginny when she told them she was going over to Nancy's house for a few minutes. Just as Ben was obsessed with his cartoon, Ginny was obsessed with cooking. She just finished making a brand-new turkey meatloaf recipe and couldn't wait to get Nancy's reaction to it.

Nancy was the ideal next-door neighbor. Besides sharing recipes, she would often lend a listening ear or be available to grab something at the market or pick up the kids from school. In a way, it was like having a sister close by. This warmed Ginny's heart, because her own sister lived two thousand miles away, and Nancy became the perfect substitute. Unfortunately, due to family, church, and work obligations, their "together" moments were sporadic, so what little time they could muster to catch up on girl talk was sacred.

Nancy washed down her bite of meatloaf with some light, dry Chablis. She never drank during the day, but this was a special occasion—the girls hadn't shared a moment together in over a month. Nancy smiled warmly at Ginny, and immediately Ginny knew her friend approved of her latest gastronomical creation. Ginny was so proud of herself.

The sound of a car door slamming brought them both back from their culinary moment. Ginny knew that it was probably Neil. As much as she would have loved to finish her visit with Nancy, she got an immediate pang in her stomach. She knew Neil would be wondering where she was, and he may not have fully appreciated the concept of running next door to share a new recipe. The friends hugged good-bye as Nancy told Ginny, "I understand. All part of the job."

Ginny sprinted across the front lawn to her house. She looked to see if Neil's truck was in the driveway. As she reached for the front door, it suddenly snapped open and little Andrew practically ran right through her. He turned and stopped, looked up at her for a moment, and continued his race down the walkway. Ginny didn't give much thought to what might be bothering the little boy. Maybe Ben said something that hurt his feelings.

Ginny entered the house and heard the television blaring way too loud. She yelled out for Ben and Neil, then grabbed the remote and turned down the sound. Instantly there was a deafening silence. Everything seemed to stand still. She walked over to the staircase and repeatedly called out their names. Nothing. Ginny's insides began to tumble. Something was wrong.

She heard a grunt upstairs, and she sprinted up the steps calling out for Neil to answer. As she reached the top landing, she was thrown back by a bloodcurdling scream coming out of Ben's room. When she looked inside the room, she saw the unthinkable. In front of her was a blood-drenched Neil holding the lifeless body of their son. Neil was staring at the ceiling screaming in agony. Bullets were strewn on the floor next to Neil's nine-millimeter revolver, the gun Ginny demanded he hide just two days earlier, so their son wouldn't play with it. But it was too late. Words were impossible, feelings immeasurable. They both tugged at the small boy's frame, begging for his life, but he was long gone.

And so began the longest day of their lives.

UNFINISHED BUSINESS

INTRODUCTION

The story you have just read is horrific—a fatal mistake. It's hard to believe that such things happen, yet they do more times than we can imagine. I have chosen this particular story because, although it is not the typical situation in which parents lose a child, it is one that has always stayed with me. There were so many layers of guilt, accusation, and shame emanating from Ginny and Neil when they came to me as clients, that it was difficult to bring their son through to them. Not only were they still deep in grief over losing Ben, but I'm sure they were running the blame game over and over in their heads. Ginny was blaming Neil for not hiding the gun in a safe place like she had asked him while at the same time feeling guilty for leaving the boys alone. Neil was blaming Ginny for leaving the boys unattended and feeling guilty for not locking up his gun. They both felt responsible for Ben's death and also felt that they had let each other down. They were going through the motion of being alive, but they were both so shut down, they seemed almost as dead as their son. When Ben came through, he had so much love and forgiveness for his parents. He tried to give them their lives back. He pleaded with them to accept his forgiveness and to forgive each other. I remember how ironic it was to hear a child say to his parents: *You have your whole lives ahead of you still. Don't keep messing them up.* When Neil and Ginny left my home, I knew they were relieved that Ben had come through, but I also knew they were caught up in whose fault it was, that they just could not get over that enormous hurdle. I heard later through mutual friends that they divorced.

It saddened me that the love and forgiveness that Ben had demonstrated from the other side wasn't enough to keep his parents together. Divorce was the last thing Ben would have wanted for Ginny and Neil. Instead of honoring their son by creating something positive out of their tragedy (like working for gun control), they perpetuated their guilt. They missed an opportunity to turn their mistake into a gift to the world by possibly stopping a similar tragedy from befalling another family. In an alternative scenario, Ginny and Neil would have stayed together, lectured to others about handgun safety, had more children, and let their love grow. Imagine how happy Ben would be to know his death was not in vain.

That is why I have written this book. I have learned a lot from the other side about how to live life, and I am continually amazed by what the spirit world has to say. Over the past twenty-five years, I have shared spirit stories through my books and demonstrations, but I am often disappointed that a spirit's advice goes unheeded. People are usually amazed when I get evidential details like a name or death scenario correct, but when a spirit offers guidance, its counsel frequently falls on deaf ears.

You see, when people shed their physical bodies at death, their spiritual selves see life from a whole new perspective. It's as if they've had Lasik surgery—they can finally do without their glasses and can see more clearly. Spirits understand why certain situations had to happen. They are able to recognize the value of others, even their enemies, and what they had to learn from them. They also realize how they could have skipped certain mistakes by not letting their egos get in the way. After crossing into the light, spirits are eager to share their newfound knowledge with the living. I am fortunate enough to be a beneficiary of many spirits' wisdom and guidance, and I am happy to share their insights with you.

So many of us obsess about the one thing that is out of our control—the past. It's the old "should've, could've, would've" approach to life. We have regrets about our jobs, our family, our money, our decisions, and our happiness. The only power we have is in the "now," and our now affects our future. We have become a society with less self-responsibility and more blame. When something goes wrong, we seek others (or God) to blame for our misfortune. When a tragedy occurs, we become angry and guilt-ridden instead of seeing the opportunity to create good from it. We replay emotional dramas that happened in our childhood or recent past; somehow thinking that life will magically change, even if we don't. Unless we overcome this mind-set, we will always feel overwhelmed by life. What are we to do?

Use this book on how to live life more graciously. Opportunity knocks every day; things can change, people can change, and you can change. It's all about being responsible for your thoughts and actions. Your thoughts have power. The life you are living right now is the result of your thoughts. Thoughts are energy—they are real things. It is because of the power of our thoughts that spirits encourage us to forgive even when it's the hardest thing to do and to push through our fears to make dreams come true. By utilizing the advice of spirits in our everyday lives, we can begin to convert conflict into peace and anger into kindness. We can stop the blame game by accepting responsibility, correcting mistakes, and turning grief into accomplishments.

We are meant to live loving lives. We are meant to have all our needs met. We are meant to express ourselves as the unique beings we are. Our spiritual friends want us to contribute to life, to be happy and to finish any unfinished business before we reach the time when we step through the threshold of light and return home.

You have already taken a step in the right direction by reading this book. Spiritual guidance is on every page. It will inspire you to go beyond what you already know. I wish you an empowered journey in claiming a life rich in love, contentment, and happiness.

PART ONE

emotional
BAGGAGE

Guilt

Every man is guilty of all the good he didn't do.

—Voltaire

My entire being focused on a single drop of liquid as it was about to plunge down into a clear mass pooled below. As the pounding in my head faded, I moved closer to the drop. Then, in an instant, I soared toward the drop, as if I were whirling on the Matterhorn ride at Disneyland. At the same time, my mind hammered me with a myriad of questions. Where am I? How did I get here? My curiosity ended as my eyes adjusted and were able to focus on the IV drip connected to a bag of saline solution next to my bed. It was obvious that I was in a hospital room, but I didn't remember what had happened to me. Was I still a part of this life, or was I somewhere else? My perceptions were strong, but somehow different.

Suddenly, I had an overwhelming feeling of being trapped—imprisoned in my own body. I opened my mouth to scream, but nothing came out. A strange cast of characters appeared before me. I had seen these faces in the past, maybe a long time ago. One face, in particular, stood out from the rest. It was a man's face, with an intense expression that seemed to bore right through me. I knew that beyond those eyes was some kind of ancient wisdom. Did he carry all of the answers to my inquiries? Did he want to divulge them to me? His face seemed to grow larger as it came closer and closer to mine. He was just about to open his mouth to speak when the locale changed.

Suddenly, I flew out a window and before me was an incredible scene of a violet, blue, pink, and orange sunset. I felt an immediate sense that the sky was expressing a joyful celebration of itself, as if its colors were alive and breathing. Then all of the hues blended together in the most delightful way to form a multitude of flower arrangements, landscapes, and rainbows rising in the background. As I attempted to understand this fascinating setting and discover its meaning for me, the man from the hospital room appeared again. This time he spoke. His words were abruptly drowned out, however, by the piercing sound of a telephone ring.

I crashed back into reality and was annoyed that I wasn't able to hear the message from the phantom male in my dream. I blindly reached for the phone and pulled it to my ear.

"Hello," I mouthed grumpily.

"Hi, James. Wake up. It's Annie from KPZ. Ready for the radio show?"

"How much time do I have?"

"About twenty minutes."

I pushed the covers aside and began my morning ritual of acknowledging the Universe for giving me another day of life and asking for God's light of protection. I tumbled into the kitchen and prepared my coffeepot for two cups of java. I pulled out a pad and pen in anticipation of the radio show. It was helpful for me to write or draw messages when spirits came through.

As I sat, waiting for the magical elixir to brew, I thought about my dream experience and could not help but speculate about its meaning.

Like most people, I have always been fascinated by dreams. They are mysterious imaginings that belong in a world all their own. Throughout my life's work as a spiritual medium, I have discovered that dreams reveal many important things to us, but we have to take the time to find out what to look for and how to use the information. For me, the first step in understanding the meaning of a particular dream is to write it down. If I don't, as time goes by I am less likely to remember the facts and images of the dream experience.

During the day when we are conscious, our psyches are bombarded by an enormous quantity of stimuli. Although we are usually unaware of all that goes on around us, our mental, emotional, physical, and spiritual selves are dramatically affected by the thoughts and images that come our way. The subconscious mind stores these stimuli, and when we sleep, it replays the impressions of the day as dreams.

Although I am not an expert in dream interpretation, I know there are various types of dreams. Some dreams display our mental and emotional anxieties as nightmares. Other dreams are symbolic, and these are usually elusive because most of us don't get the symbolism. For instance, a rat may not literally mean a rodent, but rather someone we think of as a "rat." There are also telepathic dreams. In these dreams, our loved ones who have passed over may be trying to convey a message to us.

Another type of dream is a premonition. In this dream we can actually see, feel, or experience a future event. In 1994 I dreamed of a train coming through my dining-room wall. I didn't see the train per se, but it felt like a train in the dream. The sound was loud, and the whole house shook. Wine glasses flew off shelves and shattered on the floor. Three days later, at 4:31 A.M., the Northridge Earthquake struck Los Angeles. As I ran out of my bedroom, I could see items falling off shelves and found shattered glass all over my dining-room floor. The dream I had about the train was warning me. Experiencing a real earthquake often sounds and feels like a train rattling by. One doesn't necessarily have to be a psychic to have a dream premonition.

As I stared at my blank pad, anticipating my first sip of coffee, I went over the dream images in my mind, trying to figure out their meaning. Last night's dream seemed to have affected me more than most. I felt that the ambiguous man, whoever he was, had a very strong message to give me, and I wouldn't rest until I could decipher it. I wrote in detail all the images and sights of the dream. In doing so, my mind began to wonder about consciousness, the spirit world, and the myriad of thoughts and experiences our spirits take with them when they leave the physical world at death. I thought of all the unresolved issues we leave behind, and how they hold us back from living in complete freedom and joy. Everyone, whether dead or alive, has some unfinished business. Why is this? I wondered. Why would souls choose to go through extremely traumatic experiences that shape their ideas, personalities, and lives and then leave the world without answers to their problems? Why do we hold on to painful experiences? Could there be something positive that comes out of these experiences?

The answer came quickly . . . *lessons.*

All of our life situations happen in order for us to learn. These experiences are actually gifts for the soul. The gift wrappings may not be what we would like or what we had expected, but the contents are uniquely designed just for us. The Universe is perfect, and its timing is perfect. A soul goes through life's most common and challenging emotional lessons in its quest for understanding and to move forward in its development.

My frustration grew as I tried to figure out what lessons might be learned from my dream. In the meantime, however, I had to get ready for the radio show, so I would have to wait until that night to determine if it was possible to finish my dream and get answers to my questions. The phone once again interrupted my thoughts. The show was about to begin.

IT WAS MY FAULT

"We have one of our favorite guests on the show today. He is world-renowned spiritual medium James Van Praagh. Hi, James. Welcome back to the show," said Rona. Rona was the morning deejay on one of the most popular radio shows in the country, and over the years I have been her guest many times.

Before I began the messages, as I do on any radio show, I spent a bit of time centering my energy. As soon as my eyes looked down at my pad, I focused my mind on a place of receptivity, so that I was prepared to hear, feel, or see any spirits that might be around the caller.

"Today we have Theresa on the line. Say hi to James, Theresa."

"Hi, James," Theresa replied.

As I heard the sound of the caller's voice on the other end of the phone, I locked into it to see what energies, if any, were around her. At that moment, I heard a rather high-pitched voice and received an impression. In my mind's eye I could see a young man standing right next to her left shoulder. I knew instinctively that the young man was her brother.

"Good morning, Theresa." I said. "Did your brother pass over around the age of twenty-two?"

"Yes," she said.

Her brother projected a scene onto my consciousness. It contained blood and black particles running through a human vein. Then I saw an arm lined with needle marks. The young man was crying.

"Your brother is giving me the impression that he died of a drug overdose. Is that correct?"

I could hear Theresa heave a sigh. It seemed that this validation stunned her, as if she were experiencing the agony of his death all over again. She began to cry.

"Keep breathing," I said to her.

After a few moments, she whispered, "Yes."

The spirit then impressed me with his name . . . Mark.

"Mark is telling me he is sorry. He didn't mean to go this way."

Theresa once again began crying, and then suddenly became silent.

Rona quickly jumped in. "Theresa, are you still there?"

A few seconds later Theresa let out a howl. "It was my fault. I should've stopped him. It is because of me that he died. I wanted to stop him, but I couldn't."

At that moment Mark sent thoughts to tell her to stop beating herself up about this.

I said to Theresa, "It was his choice. You had nothing to do with it. He loves you." As I conveyed the message to her, she kept crying.

She answered, "He called me that night. I knew it was him, but I couldn't pick up the phone. I knew he was probably high, and I just couldn't deal with it again."

"Who is Roger?" I asked.

The mention of Roger once again set Theresa off. "Oh my God. I can't believe it! Tell him I am so sorry. Please."

"Mark can hear your thoughts, Theresa. You can tell him directly how sorry you are."

Rona chimed in. "Do you know anyone by the name of Roger, Theresa?"

"Yes, yes, I do. Roger is an old boyfriend of mine. I introduced him to my brother. I didn't know Roger was into dealing cocaine."

Poor Theresa continued to sob. Both Rona and I tried to reassure her that everything was okay.

But Theresa continued her lament. "If I never introduced them, my brother would be alive today. Roger sold him the drugs that killed him."

I immediately said to Theresa, "Your brother wants you to know you did nothing wrong. He had to find out for himself. If you want to do something for him, please forgive yourself. He doesn't like to see you in pain."

Theresa then said, "Can you ask him what he wanted that night when he called me? I have been trying to figure it out. I should have picked up the phone."

I sent out a mental thought to Mark asking him what the phone call was all about. He showed me photographs laid out on a bed.

"He is talking about photos in a shoe box. Do you understand?"

"Yes," she responded.

"He is saying something that sounds like *purity* or *party*, no, more like *pretty*. I am not sure what this means."

Theresa reacted with recognition. "Oh God. I was the oldest sister, and I was responsible for taking care of him. When he was learning how to talk, he would look up at me and say, 'You look purrty.' He couldn't pronounce 'pretty.' He would say, 'I love you, purrty.'"

I could sense relief in Theresa's voice.

Rona interrupted, "Thank you, Theresa. We have to take another call now."

"Wait! Can I tell you one more thing?" Theresa asked.

"Yes, go ahead," said Rona.

"The photos you mentioned. Mark did keep photos in a shoe box. When they found him in his room downtown, there were photographs all over the floor of me and him when we were little kids."

I interrupted Theresa to tell her that her brother was saying at that moment, *I love you, Pretty.*

Because of the time constraints of a radio program, it is difficult to give some callers the level of help they need. There was no way Theresa's guilty feelings about her brother were going to be resolved in a few minutes on the phone. Usually, I, or someone from the radio station, will assist a caller in locating a therapist in the area.

Right after this phone call, there was a break, and I asked the station manager if I could speak off the air with Theresa.

"Her brother really needs to set her straight and is begging me to talk to her longer."

The station manager said, "Sure," and gave me Theresa's phone number.

After the show, I called Theresa, and she was still crying.

"Don't you feel better now that you've had a chance to speak with your brother?" I asked.

"Yes . . . but I still feel guilty about not being there when he needed me."

"That is something you will have to process and forgive yourself for. You can begin by looking at the situation from a bigger perspective, outside of yourself."

Then Mark began to communicate and took our conversation in quite an unexpected direction.

Tell my sister that I came back to the earth to experience one of my life lessons.

"What was it?" I asked Mark.

Mark continued. *As a soul, I had to learn about not letting substances keep me from dealing with the everyday experiences of life. I have had several prior lives in which I abused alcohol and drugs. I died of overdoses in two other lifetimes. This time I came back to see if I could beat the addictive personality that I had so often. That's what I came to do in this life. It was a test to see if I had grown.*

I conveyed this information to Theresa.

"Are you kidding me?" she asked in a frozen tone of voice.

"No. This is what he is saying."

Mark further explained. *Addiction is a tough one to learn. When you are high, you don't have to be responsible; it's the easy way out of not dealing with stresses and choices in your life. I guess I wasn't strong enough or believed in myself enough to beat it, but I tried. You do get better with each life opportunity. I will have to do it all over again, but I have promised myself that I will overcome it. By the way, thanks for all the prayers.*

Mark's profound insight left both of us in awe.

Theresa asked, "Where is he now?"

"He says he is in a place of reflection, like a hospital, but not really a hospital. He sees himself clearly as a soul and wants to help you and other people understand why he had his drug problem. He is saying, *People can start looking at drug addiction from a different point of view and perhaps show addicts more compassion.* He says that you shouldn't feel guilty about his addiction."

"Thank you, James."

"He wants to pass on one more thing. He is saying, *People should make every attempt possible to let go and heal their addictions while in the body, because they don't want to bring that memory and that yearning over here. It dirties the mind.*"

I have heard this before from spirits, and I cannot stress enough the importance of this fact. When we pass over, our cravings come with us. It is much easier to release our physical, mental, and emotional addictions in human form than as spirits, because addictions are part of our human nature, and we are more effective in breaking human habits in human bodies.

Theresa was satisfied. "My dream has come true. I spoke to my brother, and I feel better."

And with that, I said good-bye. It was a beautiful start to my day.

This reading is typical of why I *love* mediumship. It is such a healing and powerful exchange between the physical and spiritual levels. When a person has the chance to communicate with a loved one, he or she can begin to see events from a new perspective. Theresa could have spent an entire lifetime beating herself up with unnecessary guilt. However, she was afforded an opportunity to witness the bigger picture of a soul's journey and the lessons her brother chose to experience. Knowing this, Theresa would be able to heal much more quickly with her new insight about addiction. She would also be able to see people in her life as souls learning their lessons.

All types of guilt, including self-imposed guilt, can devastate us. Guilt sets us up to feel completely responsible for the outcome of a situation. I see this every day in my work. Relatives commonly wrestle with guilty feelings over the death of their dearly departed. "I should have been there at the hospital to call a nurse." "I could have kept him on the feeding tube; he might have come out of the coma." In Theresa's case, "I should have picked up the phone and saved his life."

Guilt is inherent in humans. I believe it is a type of coping mechanism, albeit a flawed one. Its purpose is to let us know that we have done something wrong. Guilt seems to be one of those things that all of us have, yet don't know how to deal with. Often we squelch it and learn to live with it. We can see the irrationality of guilt in others, because it is far easier to forgive other people's mistakes than our own. For some illogical reason, we hold ourselves up to a higher standard than we do anyone else. By understanding that guilt doesn't change anything, other than to make us feel bad, perhaps we can begin to let it go.

WHY THEM AND NOT ME?

Survivor's guilt is another prevalent form of guilt. This is guilt felt by individuals who have survived some type of catastrophe or disaster in which others have died. These survivors feel as though they have experienced good fortune at the expense of others. Many feel that they could have done something to keep the others alive. Again, this is based on an illogical belief in superhuman power. Often, survivors of a catastrophe feel unworthy and experience a fair amount of depression, sadness, numbness, and lack of interest in life.

A few years ago I led a workshop in New York City. A spirit with a great sense of humor and a twinkle in his blue eyes came through. I immediately got a sense that this spirit was with a group of guys in a cabin in the woods. They were all laughing, fooling around, and drinking shots of tequila.

"Does anyone here recognize this scenario?" I asked the crowd.

Sometimes spirits don't always know how to direct me to the person in the audience to whom their messages apply. I scanned the audience to see if I could feel any connection. I did. It was way in the back on the left side of the room. Then I had another very clear vision. A big red apple dropped from a tree into a lake and made a huge splash. I shared the image with the audience.

"Does anyone relate to this?"

There was only silence.

I know that when I receive visions as conspicuous as these, spirits have a strong message for someone. Many times I will wait until I get more information. So this time I waited.

"I am seeing a fishing line," I said to the audience. Finally, there was a murmur from the back left side of the room. A man with salt-and-pepper hair, wearing a blue and white plaid shirt, raised his hand halfway.

"Do you understand this?"

He barely spoke up. "Yeah."

"Please speak up, so we can all hear you," I said.

"Yes, I think so. I used to go fishing with my buddies at Apple Lake in upstate New York. We would rent a cabin. Could that be it?"

I knowingly smiled. "Do you understand the name Tucker?" I asked. "Tucker is a giant sort of guy with a mustache and slight paunch."

This detail got to the man in the back. He stared down at the floor and nodded his head. This was obviously disturbing to him.

"Who is Tucker?"

"My buddy . . . Jimmy Tucker."

"He wants to say hey to you. And he is not the only one. There are a bunch of guys here."

And with that remark, this poor man held his face in his hands and started crying like a baby.

The woman on his left put her arm around him and petted him. She whispered, "It'll be all right." But the man's sobs intensified as he managed to mumble a few words.

"What did you say?"

He responded in a thick New York accent. "I should be there with them. I should've saved them. I should've been with my buddies. I don't deserve to be alive."

There was an incredible hush in the room; no one knew how to react.

The scene became quite clear. A group of four men stood behind the man in the plaid shirt. I sensed that they were like one big family.

"Who is Mike or Mikey?"

The man wiped away his tears. "That's me."

The woman next to him helped him to stand up, so he could speak with me. The microphone runner also helped him to his feet and held the microphone in front of him so he could be heard.

"There are four men standing behind you, and they are laughing. *Let Mikey do it!* one of them says."

This made Mike smile.

"Yeah, they used to goof with me like that. I was the small one, and they called me Mikey. Can you tell them I'm sorry? I'm so sorry." Mike began crying again. "I can't sleep at night. I get some awful nightmares. I don't know why I am still here. I don't feel like living."

Once again the room fell silent.

One of the spirits placed an ethereal blanket on Mike's shoulders.

"Now one is covering you with a red blanket. It has a number on it."

The woman next to Mike, whom I assumed was his wife, mumbled something about a blanket.

"Yeah, I got it," he said to her.

He turned to me. "I sit with the red blanket on the patio."

"Each one of them is showing me their badges. They're policemen, aren't they? The number fourteen comes up. Was this your precinct?"

"Yeah, that's us. The fourteenth. The blanket is from there; it has the number fourteen on it. It's the only thing I kept."

I watched this bunch of guys slap Mike on the back and heard another name.

"Who is Joey Malone?"

Mike laughed. "My partner. Is he here too?"

"He is telling you to say hello to Sheila and the baby for him. He says he is fine."

"That's his wife and kid. I will tell them."

"They are showing me that you are looking at a plaque."

"I went downtown last week to look at it. I kind of felt they were there too." Mike's voice broke off.

"They are showing me the plaque."

I took a breath. "Was this the World Trade Center?"

"Yes, it was," Mike said softly.

The audience gasped.

I saw a Starbucks cup next to the plaque and asked, "Did a cup of coffee spill when you were there?"

Mike bowed his head in disbelief. "Oh my God, oh my God. Yes, I did. It was weird. I kept putting the cup back on the ledge, and it kept falling off."

"Joey says it was him. He was messing with you. He said you knew it was him."

"Holy sh——t!" Mike put his hand up to his mouth. "I'm sorry. Yeah, I knew it was him. He was always doing things like that."

He turned to his wife. "Remember? Didn't I say that to you?"

She nodded her head.

"This is unbelievable!" Mike exclaimed. Then he said with sadness, "I want to know why I'm still here. I don't want to be."

"You have to," I answered without hesitation.

The guys then gave me another message. "When you were just starting out in the force, did you save a little boy's life?"

"Let me think. Yeah, I remember. It was in a tenement uptown. I got there just in time; otherwise the kid would be dead. His father was kicking him over and over. He would have kicked him to death."

"Why don't you think of that situation?"

"I don't know . . . just never do. It happened a long time ago."

"Well, that is what they want you to know. To these guys, you saved that boy's life. If it were a choice between saving that boy or them, they would have wanted you to save the boy."

Mike looked at me. "I don't get it. What has one got to do with the other?"

I could barely keep up with the thoughts flying into my mind, and I had to speak quickly to get it all out.

"You are going to have another opportunity to save lives. You're here because you still have work to do. That's your soul's plan. You need to be in a particular place, because you will save two women. These women are doctors, and they will accomplish great things. So you see, you never know the reason why certain things occur. There is a higher order to things, even though we are unaware of it."

Mike looked stunned, as did many in the audience. I was also dazed.

"Thank you," Mike said. He seemed to have grown two feet taller with this prediction. "I hope that's the case. Tell them I understand."

I turned to the audience. "We never know what is waiting for us right around the corner or the opportunities afforded us in which we can influence or help others."

I assured Mike that his buddies heard every word he said. "They know every thought you have too."

I described their actions to Mike. "They're tossing a pitcher of beer over your head."

Mike laughed. "That's amazing. The last time we were all together, we were playing softball, and we won. We celebrated at the bar, and the next thing I knew, they were dumping a pitcher of beer on my head. Unbelievable! Hey, could you tell them one more thing?"

"Sure."

"Tell them I love them. They're the best guys around. And tell Joey to get the hell out of my dreams, would ya?"

The audience laughed.

And so began Mike's road to healing.

This is another example of how people beat themselves up with guilty feelings. In Mike's case, he couldn't see the good he had done, but looked only at what he couldn't do.

So what exactly is guilt's function and what does it motivate us to do? Freud thought guilt served to effectively regulate social behavior. If people didn't feel guilty, so the argument goes, they would be much less likely to care about hurting other people's feelings or damaging their property. In other words, guilt motivates us to act good; otherwise we would all be transgressors. Another theory has to do with punishment. We must punish the guilty when they do wrong and heal the social damage done. That's all well and good, but, unfortunately, innocent people often punish themselves for not doing anything wrong.

A third type of guilt, which I run into all the time, is the guilt that is imposed on one person by another. Most of the time I deal with the living who feel guilty about how they treated a deceased person or the fact that they didn't do enough for that person. However, occasionally spirits express guilt for inflicting their wants and needs on someone else when they were alive. In order for these spirits to move on to the higher spheres of the heavenly worlds, they need to make amends with their loved ones on earth.

YOU ARE STUPID

The following reading was done before members of my monthly Spirit Circle in southern California. As with all my demonstrations, I never know what will happen beforehand, so I am just as surprised at those who show up as the audience. As I tell my students, some spirits are better at manipulating the energy spheres in order to connect with the living, and some spirits have greater desire and intention to get their messages across.

"There is a lady standing behind a gentleman here on the side, and she won't be quiet. She is very powerful and is demanding to speak."

As I pointed to seventy-three-year-old Bryan Patterson, he slumped down into his seat. I knew the old guy was a bit embarrassed that he had been targeted.

"Sir, may I come to you?"

"I'm just here to watch," he said.

I surmised that Bryan had come out of curiosity and had not expected to be the recipient of a message.

"There is a woman standing behind you wearing a red sweater. Her arms are crossed in front of her. She is pretty insistent that I come to you with her message."

"Oh boy. What does she want?"

There were some chuckles from the audience.

"She is talking about Virginia, not the name, but the place. Did you live there?"

"No."

"She is saying you did. She is calling you *stupid*. She keeps repeating, *You're stupid!*"

"Oh, she always did that. It was her nickname for me." Bryan smiled. However, the rest of the crowd seemed uncomfortable.

"Now let me think . . ." He looked at the woman on his left side. She looked back at him with a puzzled expression.

"Yes, we did live in Virginia. We moved down to Richmond to stay with her father before he died."

The feisty spirit woman then moved right up to me and stared at my face. She was very desperate to get her message across. I telepathically reassured her that I would. Then I told her to back away from me if she wanted my help.

"This woman is saying that she was your wife Mollie. Was this a second marriage?" I asked.

"Yes. I was married twice. She was my second wife." Bryan thought a bit. "Well, she was my second, and I was her third."

"She is speaking about Marie. Mollie won't stop about Marie. She says she didn't like Marie."

"She really didn't know Marie," replied Bryan.

"She is telling me that Marie was in her way. Now she is showing me Florida."

Mollie became even more insistent.

"She wants me to make sure that you understand what she's saying. Do you understand this?"

"Oh, yes, I do."

Bryan was a very sweet man. He seemed like the kind of man who wouldn't hurt a fly.

"Sir, if I may be so bold," I continued, "I don't feel that you and this Mollie really were equals."

"Many others have said the same thing."

"What is her problem with this Marie?" I asked. "She is talking about something she did to Marie and something about moving to Florida."

Bryan tried to explain. "I met Mollie while I was still married to Marie."

Many in the audience nodded. We got the picture. Mollie was the other woman.

Bryan continued, "Mollie and I worked together, and we got to seeing one another. Mollie fell in love with me and used to tell me how terrible Marie was and that Marie was lying to me."

"Do you think Marie would have lied to you?" I asked, seeing and feeling where this communication was going.

Bryan looked down at the floor. "Ah, well, no. I don't think she ever did. I know she didn't. But Mollie didn't like her."

Suddenly, Mollie began talking about three kids. "Did you have three children? Mollie is saying you did."

"Yes, Marie and I had three children. But I left them to live in Florida with Mollie. She didn't like kids."

The audience muttered their disapproval. It was clear that Mollie broke up a nice family home.

"I see." As I watched this spirit in front of me, I realized the effect of her actions on many people's lives. Mollie too had realized how she had affected the lives of a family for her own selfish gain. She began to cry right in front of me. Her seemingly demanding personality began to waver. At that moment, I felt compassion for her.

"Mollie is giving me the impression that she was a tough lady. She felt that she was superior to you, and you were subservient to her. She told me that you used to do everything for her—anything that she demanded. Oh my goodness, she tells me that you used to do all the laundry, shopping, cooking, and cleaning, while she stayed in bed and watched television and read magazines. Is all this correct?"

Bryan was embarrassed. "Is she ashamed of me? I tried to do the best I could for her. I loved her and would do anything for her."

Everyone in the room was shocked, including me. It was not the reaction we were expecting.

The biggest surprise of the evening was still to come.

"The reason Mollie came here tonight is not only for your benefit," I said to Bryan. I began to receive an overwhelming sense of grief from this spirit.

"Bryan, Mollie came here tonight to let you know that she is sorry. She is very sorry for what she did."

"Really? She never said she was sorry, ever. Are you sure you got her?" he asked.

"Yes, I'm sure."

At this point Mollie began sending me her feelings, thoughts, and images very quickly. They were everything that she failed to show to Bryan when they were together.

"She feels extremely guilty about how she treated you in life. She is telling me that she didn't see what she was doing to you and didn't ever take the time to see your enormous capacity for kindness until she left this world. Mollie is telling me that she should have known that you were her teacher during her lifetime. You were brought into her life, so that she could see how someone could share love unconditionally, with no strings attached. You loved her, no matter how she treated you. She is sorry that she lied to you and is feeling terribly guilty about ruining your life and your relationship with your children."

Tears rolled down Bryan's face. "Deep down, I did know the truth, but I felt sorry for Mollie. I wanted her to experience love."

"Have you recently been invited to a family reunion?" I asked.

Bryan responded, "Yes. How did you know that? I am going next week to see my three kids. It's been a while since I've seen them."

"Mollie is sorry that she lied to you about Marie. She felt that she forced you to divorce Marie. You were her security blanket in a way. She is telling me that Marie never lied. She feels a lot of guilt and shame about her lies. She wants you to please convey her deepest apologies to Marie."

Bryan replied, "She can tell Marie herself. She is sitting right here."

He turned to the white-haired woman whose hand he had been clutching during the entire reading.

Everyone gasped. They were on the edge of their seats anticipating Marie's side of the story.

Marie spoke. "I understand. Tell her that she doesn't have to feel guilty anymore. Actually, Mollie brought Bryan and me closer together. We have learned so much about each other because of her. We share so much now because of what happened. Our children have also taught us. We are very grateful to be with each other at this time of life."

With Marie's words of forgiveness, the harsh features of Mollie's face changed. I could see her turn younger and softer. I knew she was free to move on. She thanked me, and I acknowledged her.

All the people in the room got on their feet and gave Bryan and Marie a standing ovation.

So what is the first step in recognizing guilt and knowing its purpose? Look at your life and ask yourself: What makes me feel guilty? Is it a relationship? Perhaps you spend more time at work than with your family. Your feeling of guilt might mean that you need to change your behavior. If you choose to ignore the problem, you might suffer consequences. But if you listen to your feeling, you might change your behavior for the better. In this instance, the feeling of guilt has been helpful.

Once you realize a behavior change is in order, a good first step is apologizing. But it's easy to apologize. The next step is a bigger one—actually taking action and changing behavior. We want to learn the lesson and not have to repeat it. Once we recognize the problem and deal with it, we are able to move on with our lives. We don't need to obsess about it; we can make our amends, learn, and move on.

Feeling guilty for things we cannot change is a different matter. Whether in this life or in the afterlife, guilt can weigh heavily on our souls and grip us so tightly that we are unable to move on. When we cannot change a situation because we have no control over it, we must let go of our self-condemnation. Guilt can quickly turn into regret and self-pity. The only way out is through acceptance and, as Marie showed us, forgiveness.

TWO

Regrets

I'd rather look forward and dream,
than look backward and regret.

—Anonymous

Regret, like guilt, keeps us focused on the past. Have you ever looked in the mirror and thought to yourself: What am I doing here? Is this really my life? What would have happened if I hadn't moved away from home? What if I told that person what I really thought of her? Why am I afraid of what people think of me? Would my life circumstances be better if I had moved to another city? Would I be happier if I had remained married or had gotten a divorce?

Like guilt, regret is also a part of the human experience. The word "regret" originates from the Middle English word *regreet*, meaning "to lament" or "to feel sorry," which is from the Old English word *graetan*, meaning "to weep." Our regrets may serve as wonderful opportunities from which we can learn, or they may become slayers of our self-esteem and hold us back from future opportunities. When we rehash our past decisions over and over in our minds, we can create regrets that corrode our present lives.

We all come to a point in life when we look at our existence with some sort of regret. "If I hadn't quit that job, I could have been a vice president by now." "If I had married for love instead of money, I would have been better off." Getting older gives us a broader perspective to evaluate our past choices, including the consequences of our mistakes. Most of us are left with deep longings for missed opportunities.

Where does regret come from? My first thought is that regret stems from lost experiences. In hindsight, we feel we missed a chance to do something wonderful or meaningful. A regret can also be a dream that we denied ourselves. Say you wanted to be a ballerina, but couldn't afford years of dance lessons. Or you wanted to play ball in the big leagues, but didn't have the power to hit the ball far enough. There might have been things you could have done to improve your resources and abilities, but time and life's circumstances pulled you away from achieving those dreams.

Another type of regret besets people who are afraid to take risks. Perhaps they don't have enough self-esteem to believe in themselves. Perhaps they fear responsibility, especially for making decisions or doing the necessary work to succeed. These individuals may regret taking the easy way out, never testing themselves or their abilities. They may fall into an emotional slump and be overcome with self-pity, resentment, anger, and depression. In many cases, they live out the rest of their lives as bitter, cynical people.

Still another type of regret is formed when we recall how we treated others. "I didn't have to yell at my child so much when she was growing up." "I could have been more helpful to my neighbor when he got sick." "I wish I had gotten more involved when my nephew had a drinking problem."

Most regrets have to do with family ties. So much of the work I do involves mending separations between family members. An argument turns into a feud that lasts years. The relationship is ruined because no one will concede; no one will say, "I'm sorry." A feud between two family members can have a toxic effect on the rest of the family. It's no fun being in the middle between a brother and a sister or a mother and a son who are at odds. Also, there is a lot of awkwardness and sadness at holidays. Who do you invite to Thanksgiving dinner? Who do you visit at Christmas or Hanukkah? When family members cannot work out their differences, the only thing they have to look forward to is distrust, disrespect, and isolation. I have communicated thousands of messages to family members from their loved ones in spirit. Almost all, on both sides of the veil, regretted lost moments of family togetherness because of their narrow-mindedness and stubbornness.

The good news is that we can do something to get rid of regrets and change our lives for the better. First of all, we must know that we are powerless over the past. The past is gone, and we cannot get it back. We can only live in the present moment. Now is the time to weigh our current circumstances, reevaluate our values and goals, and begin to make decisions that will foster the lives we want to live.

THE BIBLE TELLS ME SO

A beautiful young woman, Jenny Haustead, was the perfect image of an American wife and mother. Jenny was proud of her family's hundred-year-old heritage in the small South Carolina town where she grew up. A wonderfully mannered, charming, blonde, blue-eyed attractive woman, Jenny could have been a cover model for *Ladies Home Journal*. At the least, she was homecoming queen in high school. Jenny's fashion sense was flawless, and strangers often asked her where she did her shopping. Even her hair was arranged to perfectly frame her lovely face. Nothing was out of place. Jenny always thought that making a good impression was important, because that's how most people judged you. Jenny spent her days homeschooling her two boys, Doug and Bobby, and she never missed a Sunday church service. From all outward appearances, Jenny had the ideal life, but it would soon start coming apart at the seams.

If we fast-forward sixteen years, we can catch up with Jenny and her family. The following reading shows exactly how stubbornness and regret can create enormous heartache.

I looked over at a woman in her mid-fifties. She was on the aisle seat of the sixth row to my left. During the evening, several spirits gave messages to many of the people in her row, and every time I spoke I noticed a good-looking, young man's spirit standing behind one particular woman at the end of the row. The spirit did not offer any message, but rather stared at me, wondering if I could detect his presence.

Finally, I felt as though I had to talk to this spirit. I looked at the middle-aged woman on the aisle and asked her, "Do you know a blond man who died around the age of twenty-six?"

"No, I don't think so," she replied.

With that answer, the young man thanked me for acknowledging him. I felt his excitement and knew that he didn't want to miss the opportunity to convey what he had wanted to say for a very long time. He began to send me his thoughts.

"Do you know the name Jen or Jenny? This man is telling me this. He is also talking about sailing, and the name Bob or Rob."

"Oh, God. Yes. The sailing. That is my nephew Robert, Bobby, my sister Jenny's son. Is he here? Oh my God. I'm so sorry, Bobby." The middle-aged woman broke down and cried.

"Do you know a Chris or Christine, please?"

"Yes. I'm Christine."

"You've had dreams of Bobby, haven't you?" I asked.

"Yes, but they're more like nightmares. I should have . . ."

"He is telling me you weren't there when he died. He said you were back east and did not get to the hospital in time."

Christine was shocked to hear me tell her something only few knew. She looked down at her lap and covered her eyes.

"He wants you to know that he didn't die alone. He says you were worried about that."

Suddenly the woman looked up at me. "He didn't? Oh, thank God. I'm sorry I wasn't there for you, Bobby."

"Do you know his mom?" I asked.

"Yes, of course. She is my sister. What is he saying?"

Bobby suddenly gave me a very strong feeling. "I feel that Bobby's mom would not like what I am doing. She does not approve of this sort of communication. It goes against her beliefs. Is that right?"

"Yes, he's right. She's very religious."

"He is asking me to please pass on a message to her. He says that he completely forgives her and that she no longer needs to hold on to her regrets. The regrets have taught her enough, and she needs to let them go. He is very proud of her, and she is too smart to follow fearful and limited beliefs.

"I'll tell her."

It was interesting that Bobby then showed me the Bible.

"Are you familiar with the Bible, and in particular the passage Leviticus 18:22?" I asked.

"I do, unfortunately. That was the main passage Jenny used against Bobby for being gay. She was a born-again Christian. She believed that Bobby was living in sin. Because of her strict beliefs, she felt that Bobby was going against God's will."

Christine added, "She tried getting Bobby deprogrammed, exorcised, you name it. She tried everything, but Bobby was still Bobby. He couldn't change who he was, and he was such a great kid. Unfortunately, he was discovered having sex with his high-school volleyball coach. That was when Jenny's perfect world collapsed. Finally, she told him that if he continued to live his sinful lifestyle, she would disown him. He continued, and she stopped knowing him."

I couldn't believe what I was hearing. "How long ago was this?"

"About sixteen years," Christine replied. "After that, the floodgates opened. Jenny marched in protests with her church whenever gay events took place in the city. Then Bobby got sick and died."

"Bobby is telling me that after his passing his mother started to understand."

"Yes, after he died, Jenny began to examine her beliefs. She pored through the Bible, researching it with various scholars, and soon began to realize that she had been told the wrong information."

Christine continued. "The more Jenny studied, the more she felt betrayed by her religious beliefs. She realized that her son was not a sinner. Yet because her church condemned him, she condemned him too. Since then, Jenny has been so full of regret. She wanted to make amends to her son and do something to remember him by."

"What did she do?" I asked.

"Jenny is an AIDS activist and travels all around the country teaching love instead of hate."

"Is she still involved with the same Christian church?"

"Oh, no. She is with a new church that accepts gay people. She says they preach love, not judgment. She says she feels closer to God now than she ever had before."

Bobby was crying tears of love. He had one more message to pass on. "He is saying, *Tell Mom I love her.*"

Like Jenny, we have regrets when we lose loved ones before we have had a chance to say good-bye or make amends over shattered feelings. It is not easy to go through the rest of our lives with unanswered questions like "What would have happened if . . . ?"

As I have said, when regret is not dealt with in a positive manner, it can devastate the rest of your life. I have received thousands of letters from people around the world who actually suffer from their regrets on a daily basis. They attempt to live somewhat normal lives, but until their situation is dealt with in a healthy and constructive way, they are only masking their pain.

It is vital for everyone to understand the exact ramifications of carrying regrets from this life into the next. We must free ourselves of this emotional roadblock and heal here. When regrets are not dealt with on earth, they become a part of our spirits' psyches and haunt us in the other world.

Since spirits reside in a very mental world, all feelings and thoughts are amplified, and any emotional debris that they bring with them is exaggerated. The behavior they have chosen in their earthly life becomes magnified in the spirit world. I have often said, everyone will see you exactly as you are. You cannot hide your thoughts and emotions in the spirit world. Your character distinctions and personality traits parade out in the open for all to see; you are mentally and emotionally naked. Understanding this, you might reevaluate your unmovable positions while still alive on earth and bring a new perspective to the choices you make, because unfortunately when you die, you will not be rid of the problem you were unwilling to face on earth. My best advice is to reconcile your differences now.

Just imagine how awful it is for spirits in a heightened state of reality to feel their earthly regrets. Often I hear spirits moan, *If only I knew this when I was alive, I would have behaved very differently.* Spirits often express feelings that go beyond just being sorry. They beg those of us on earth for forgiveness and compassion, so that they can let go of their emotional baggage and move on to the next stage in their evolution.

And for that very reason, I am trusting that you, readers, will take it upon yourselves to learn from others' heartaches, pains, and regrets and apply that knowledge to your own life. You don't have to suffer from unfinished business when you leave this life. You can be free.

The following spirit communication shows the type of pain to which I refer. The spirit was so sorry for what he did to others while he lived on earth; regrettably, like so many others, he realized too late that his actions destroyed so many people's lives.

SAVANNAH SAVINGS

One summer evening, I was in the Southeast doing a demonstration. It was a large group, about 40 percent men and 60 percent women, a demographic that has drastically changed over the years. When I first started doing public workshops, it was usually 80 percent women. The other 20 percent were usually husbands dragged along by their wives. Times have indeed changed.

I was about to call for a break when a spirit wearing a gray suit kept pointing to a woman in the audience. He told me his name was Earl.

"Excuse me, ma'am," I said to the woman, who looked about seventy-five. "Do you know the name Earl?"

The woman stared at me, listening intently to every word I said.

"No, I don't know of anyone with that name."

"He is talking about Savannah Savings," I said.

Instantly, the woman's whole demeanor changed. "Oh, that SOB? I read that he died. Well, I hope he rots in hell!"

The audience was aghast at this woman's callous remark. I could hear people grumbling throughout the room. The man sitting to this woman's right whispered something in her ear.

As I took in all of this, Earl stood in front of me shaking his head from side to side. *She won't listen to me. I came in hopes that I could let her know how I feel.*

I looked over at the woman and asked, "What's your name?"

"Trudy!" she shouted.

The man next to her made an effort to quiet her.

"This man Earl is saying, *Please ask this lovely lady to find it in her heart to forgive me. I am so sorry about what happened.*"

Trudy didn't bat an eye at his plea. "He should feel bad after what he did. What a crook! He stole everything we had left. All of our re-tirement money and savings. Gone! I am not the only one; there are plenty more he did it to."

While Trudy was speaking, the man next to her put his arm around her shoulders.

Earl was genuinely upset as he proceeded to fill me in on what hap-pened. *I owned a company with a group of partners. My job was to get investors, and their job was to invest the money. I was good at getting the people.*

"He is saying he had a gift with people."

Trudy interrupted. "Big deal! What are we supposed to do now, Earl?"

"Earl is saying that he's terribly sorry, Trudy, and that he regrets everything. He didn't know at the time that the investments were bad. He says that it wasn't part of his job. He is reliving every moment of his existence feeling the pain he has caused others. He asks himself over and over how he could have done it differently. He is so upset that he ruined so many lives. He wants you to believe him; he didn't mean to hurt anyone. He couldn't see then what he can see now. He says, *I have to make amends for my actions.*"

Earl went on to describe that he was in some sort of therapy station.

"He is showing me his circumstances. I see him in a dimly lit at-mosphere. It's filled with a heaviness created by his greedy energy. He is not alone. Other people like him are there. They have similar atti-tudes and behaviors. Lots of darkness and misery."

"Sounds like hell to me," Trudy said smugly.

"I guess you can say that."

I did my best to explain what I saw and felt to the rest of the crowd. "On that side of life, Earl is learning how his fear, greed, and insatiable desires blinded him. He believed that accumulating money was more important than anything, and that idea eventually became his truth. Now that he is experiencing the world that he created, he literally feels blocked up by his own greediness and materialism. His soul must not only suffer for his thoughts and actions; he must feel the agony of those he wronged. He has a lot of work to do."

The audience had been silent and intent as they listened to this spirit's story.

I turned to address the woman in front of me once again. "Trudy, although you knew this man only by the way he affected you, you must think of a bigger picture at work."

Earl then went on about his life as a child. "He is telling me his life story now. He was always getting beat up and put down by his two older brothers. Because of this, he grew up with a severe lack of confidence. He says that if he ever showed it, his brothers made sure to knock it out of him. He wanted his father and brothers to think of him as a somebody. He just wanted them to love and accept him."

"Why are you going on about all this?" asked Trudy. "I don't care what happened to him."

I explained, "Sometimes we need to know a person's background in order to understand his motivation." I sighed. "Do you think you can find some compassion for him in this situation? He has been trying to help you and Joe."

Trudy was taken by surprise at the mention of Joe, but she snapped back. "Joe doesn't need his help, especially now."

Then Earl sent me a new thought. "Are you familiar with a Dr. Watkins?"

"Yes, that's my dad's doctor," responded the man next to Trudy. He introduced himself as her son, Steven. All this time, Steven had been sitting back in his chair appearing quite skeptical about what I was saying.

I said to Steven, "Earl is telling me that your father almost died, because the doctors at the hospital misdiagnosed him. Is that right?"

"How do you know this?" Steven questioned.

"This Dr. Watkins walked right into your father's room, didn't he?"

As I described what Earl was explaining to me, Steven turned white.

"This Dr. Watkins thought he was on the seventh floor, but he was on the sixth. He went into your father's room thinking that he was seeing some other patient. When Dr. Watkins examined your father, he immediately discovered what was wrong with him. None of the other doctors could figure out what Dr. Watkins figured out—that he had an allergic reaction in his lungs."

There was a sound of surprise from the audience.

Steven remarked, "We wondered how this complete stranger could walk into Dad's room and give the correct diagnosis. It didn't make any sense at the time. We figured our prayers were answered and this doctor had been sent from heaven."

The crowd oohed.

"Yes, he was," I confirmed. "It was Earl who influenced the doctor to get off at the wrong floor and visit your dad."

"No way!" Steven called out.

"I believe it!" yelled Trudy. "If he can persuade us to give him all our money, why couldn't he persuade a doctor to go where he wants him to?"

Everyone laughed.

I could tell that Trudy's hard shell was beginning to soften. She finally understood that Earl wasn't really a bad person, just someone caught up in bad circumstances.

She looked at her son and then at me. "Tell Earl not to worry anymore. I forgive him." She hesitated. "Can you tell him one more thing?"

"Yes."

"Thank him for giving me back my Joe!"

"Oh, he hears you, Trudy."

I asked the audience to send Earl love and forgiveness, so that he could move out of the darkness and into the light. I also told Trudy

how proud I was of her for forgiving this man. Then I took a much-
needed break.

THE BIG SECRET

Much too often I see how the seeds of hate, abuse, and neglect are
sown in children. The early years of life shape our sense of who we are
and all our future actions. Children look to adults to take care of them
and protect them. However, when adults have no concept of right and
wrong because they were not taught it by their parents, the end results
are nothing less than devastating. It is heartbreaking that humans treat
each other so badly.

During my spirit communications, I am acutely aware of spirits as
human beings. I am able to decipher their once human natures, some
of which are extremely hurtful. Nevertheless, I do feel intense compassion for most of them. It is so easy to judge another, because judgment
places us in a position of power. When we love ourselves for who we
are and love others for exactly who they are, there is very little reason
to judge.

It constantly amazes me how spirits can assist us in expanding our
understanding while we journey on earth. From the following spirit
communication, I hope you will look at this very disturbing situation
with a new awareness.

"What is your name, please?" I asked the pretty blonde woman
sitting mid-aisle.

"Cassandra, but everyone calls me Sandy."

As I tuned into Sandy's energy field, I was instantly aware of her
multilayered aura. From her neck up she had beautiful emanations of
gold, blue, and pink. This meant she had a great capacity to love and
could apply that to spirituality if she so chose.

Usually when my spirit guides tell me to scan a person's aura, it is
so I can see how he or she is holding on to an old pattern, a past hurt,

or an emotional trauma. If this past hurt goes untreated, it can affect the health of the physical, mental, spiritual, and emotional bodies. In Sandy's case, it was very obvious to me that something was amiss. I saw something in her aura that I see way too often. In her midsection, from below her heart to the top of her belly button, I saw muted colors of brown and gray. The vibrations of these colors were very slow and sluggish. I knew that the colors in this area are supposed to be green and yellow and the rate of vibration much higher. When I saw the darker colors in Sandy, I knew that she was emotionally closed down. Something had happened to Sandy, and she was afraid to feel.

I confronted her. "Sandy, you are a person who has great ideals, but you are afraid to let anyone in emotionally. Would you say that is true?"

"Yes, I guess so." She gave a nervous laugh. "Could be."

I tuned into her on a deeper level. "You were hurt a long time ago by someone you trusted. You put your trust in this person, and he abused it. Correct?"

"I don't know. Doesn't that happen to everyone?" she questioned.

"No, not necessarily," I responded. Then I became aware of a swirling energy to her left side that manifested itself as a man. I felt that he was connected to this situation and that he was either her father or an uncle. I received an impression from this spirit.

"Do you know the name Alfred?" I asked.

Sandy looked down. I knew that he was the last person she was expecting to hear from, and the one she did not want to hear from. Her eyes began to swell with tears, and her face turned a bright red.

She did not answer, so I repeated the question. "Do you know Alfred?"

"Yeah, he is my father's brother. My uncle Alfred."

I could tell she was very uncomfortable speaking about him.

"He wants to give love to the family and tells me that December was significant."

"He died in December."

Then very suddenly Alfred showed me images and wanted me to convey these to her.

"He is showing me a pocket watch and a staircase. Do you understand?"

These images took Sandy by complete surprise. She was staring straight at me, and I could tell that I hit a nerve.

"F——k him, and the horse he rode in on!" she shouted.

I was not used to hearing this kind of reaction, but as with Trudy in the previous reading, an angry reaction is often rooted in deep hurt.

I mentally asked Alfred, "Why are you here, please?"

He mentally answered, *To heal her heart. I am responsible. I have to do the right thing.*

Sandy was watching me talk to the spirit. "Is he telling you about the staircase and the watch? Huh?"

"No, he isn't."

I did get an overpowering feeling that this guy was extremely ashamed. "He wants me to tell you that he is sorry. He doesn't think you will understand, but he is sorry."

"Sorry? Are you kidding me? Doesn't he realize that he screwed me up for life? I haven't had a decent relationship . . ." Sandy's voice dropped.

The audience sat silently, waiting to hear more.

Sandy lifted her face. "And the men I pick either hit me or abuse me in some way. That's all thanks to good old Uncle Alfred."

I was amazed at how candidly Sandy spoke in front of a bunch of strangers, but I also knew that this reading could be healing not only for Sandy, but also for other members of the audience who could relate to her experience.

Alfred kept repeating, *Tell her how sorry I am.*

I tried to relay this to Sandy, but she didn't want to hear it.

"Do you know what the pocket watch and the staircase mean?" she asked.

I knew she was determined to tell us whether we wanted to hear it or not.

"Every Saturday night my parents went out. My Uncle Alfred would babysit my brother and me. After my brother fell asleep, my uncle asked me if I wanted to wind his pocket watch. I told him yes. He said if I was a good girl, I would find it sitting on the shelf in the closet under the stairs. Do you understand? My uncle would touch me . . ." Again her voice trailed off.

"How long did this go on?" I asked. "Did you tell anyone about it?"

"Five years, and *no*, I told *no one*, and I have regretted not telling my family. It was supposed to be a secret, and I kept it inside me my whole life."

"Didn't anyone notice or suspect?"

"I don't know, and I don't care," Sandy said with such bitterness in her voice.

Alfred mentally sent me several thoughts. "He wants you to understand that when he was a young child he was molested, and he associated love with the abuse."

"I really don't care. He should have known better if it happened to him."

Abuse is a very difficult issue to deal with and to heal from.

"Well, maybe this is a beginning. At least you are talking about it. The more you uncover the hurt and pain, the more you can put it behind you."

Sandy sat quietly this time, thinking about what I just said.

Alfred kept sending me his thoughts. "He is terribly sorry to have hurt you. He wants you to please try and understand."

"I don't know if I can. I should have told someone, but I didn't know how. I have regretted not saying anything."

"You were a little girl. Don't punish yourself for what happened."

Then Alfred gave me an impression of a car flying through the air.

"Was Alfred in a car accident? Is that how he died?"

"Yeah, he was drunk and drove off the road."

"Did he go over a cliff?" I asked.

"Yes, as a matter of fact, he did."

Then an unusual thought came over me that I had to relay. "Sandy, your uncle is telling me that he wasn't drunk during the car accident."

"No? So what?"

"He is telling me that he was so ashamed, he couldn't live with himself for hurting you. He killed himself on purpose."

"What?" she voiced her shock.

"He wanted you to know that you are not the only damaged person. He brings you his heart and is asking for your understanding."

With those final words, Sandy broke down and wept from deep within. Her tears were years in the making, and with every sob the brown and gray energies around her faded a little more.

There are many kinds of regrets, beginning with unimportant day-to-day regrets, like not calling someone on her birthday or not buying a stock before it rose in value. Bigger regrets include things like not taking a certain job or not saying something when a friend tells a racist joke. Then there are the biggest regrets, like the ones we just encountered.

Regrets can fester inside us, causing a lifetime of misunderstanding and judgment, and keeping us in a constant state of stress and grief. Regret hangs out in our auras; it causes so many problems on so many levels. If we could see how regret clouds our reasoning, decisions, and spiritual insight, we would decide to release what we cannot change and make peace with ourselves.

Even the most grievous offenses can be forgiven. As in Sandy's case, the mere opening to a new awareness helped her to let go of her regret. With compassion for her uncle, who had suffered similar circumstances, she was on her way to repairing the hole created in her soul. Ultimately, Sandy would have to find it in her heart to forgive and love herself and feel worthy. These are the necessary ingredients for complete healing.

THREE

Love Versus Fear

*When the power of love overcomes the love of power,
the world will know peace.*

—Jimi Hendrix

A week had gone by since I had my profound and mysterious dream, and even though time had passed, the dream still haunted me. Each night before falling asleep, I had attempted through meditation to connect with it once again. I was eager to see if there was some message behind it that I might have missed. It seemed I did miss something at the time. One of the most frustrating aspects of my work is that, although I am able to reach beyond earthly dimensions and bring through messages for others, I cannot do it for myself. Many psychics share this common trait. Therefore, I count on my dreams to bring me insights from my guides and loved ones. I have found that, indeed, dreams are a proven vehicle for spirits to make themselves known. So, even though I was unable to get back into my core dream to find its meaning, I remained open that something would still reveal itself.

As I went back in my head trying to dissect the dream, I recalled the main images I saw. I knew that I was in some kind of a hospital.

I had seen a beautiful sunset that turned into lovely flower arrangements. Then there was the mystery man. What was he trying to tell me?

The sunset looked familiar to me. I had seen something like it in waking life. Could it be the kind of sunset I sometimes see from my house on a crisp winter evening? Or could I have seen such a sunset in a place I had been to earlier in my life? I had no idea, but it seemed to be vaguely familiar.

Why was I in a hospital environment? Was this a symbol for healing? I didn't want to overanalyze it, because a dream has a lot to do with our emotional content. I vividly remember that I had an overwhelming feeling of love and caring in the dream. It was pure love, and it made me happy. I also sensed that it had something to do with a new beginning, especially because the flower arrangements came to life.

But the mystery man had me stumped. What was he trying to tell me? At this point, I thought I was taking this dream too literally. Dreams are usually symbolic. Did this man represent some part of me? I could not let go of this dream; it had become deeply imbedded in my consciousness. I had decided to review it again at another time. Maybe a light would go off, and some new thoughts or feelings would come to me.

The most important sense I got from the dream was love, and I would keep my mind focused on that. Love is the one force, the one energy, of which we are all made. It is through this force, love, that I am able to bridge the space between the spirit side of life and the physical world. Love is who we are; it is the equivalent of life itself. In my workshops, I often use the phrases "God is Love" and "Love is God." To me, they are one and the same; we cannot separate one from the other. God always says yes, but our egos say no.

As the banker from the last chapter's reading soon realized, having a fortune is not the answer. Many of us try to hold on to love as if it's a possession, but love cannot be possessed. Love is expansive; it cannot be fitted into the limitations of our human consciousness. I always find it interesting to watch couples try to impose their idea of love on one another. For instance, a woman may try desperately to manipulate her mate into her picture of ideal love. But she is setting herself up for heartache, because her partner can never be what she considers *perfect* love. It would be so much better if she could celebrate her partner for exactly who he is and appreciate the uniqueness of their special love.

We come together to learn various levels and aspects of love, for love is never static, but always evolving. Love is simultaneously random and ordered, so intangible and yet a part of everything, and when we attempt to limit it or categorize it, we get into trouble.

The opposite of love is fear. If there were no love, there would only be fear. Whenever there is an absence of love, it feels unnatural to us. Think of the last time you had a quarrel with someone. Your blood pressure rose, your body temperature changed, you felt shaky and out of balance. You felt very uncomfortable. Unfortunately, there is more fear in the world than love. Too many people are at war with one another on so many levels, and the effect is totally jarring. It goes against everything that is natural to us as spiritual beings. If God is Love, then fear is a false god, and if we believe in fear, then we worship a false idol.

THE HEART'S UNLIMITED SUPPLY OF LOVE

When there is a committed love bond between two people on a soul level, the connection is extremely strong. This bond transcends the veil and goes beyond the death of the human body. Out of my thousands of readings, this next one in particular sticks in my mind.

One Friday night I was conducting a workshop in North Hollywood, California. Before it began and while people were taking their seats, I went into another room to prepare myself. It is rare for a spirit to disturb me before an event, but sometimes it will happen. As I ran my energy up my spine to the throat center, I clearly heard the voice of a woman saying, *Please help my Frankie. He has lost his way.* I sent a thought to this female spirit to give me her name. *Karen* was the reply. Karen impressed upon me that she was Frankie's wife.

I often keep a pad and pen with me, so that I can quickly jot down any details when a spirit comes through with a message. This night was no exception. I wrote down the names Frankie and Karen on my pad. Then I told Karen that I would be open to speaking with her when I started the message part of my workshop. That seemed to be fine with her, and I finished my preliminary preparation work.

About an hour later, when I began receiving messages from spirits, I clearly heard Karen say, *I'm here. Please help my Frankie!*

I asked the crowd, "Is there a Frankie here? You lost your wife, Karen."

Immediately a man in the last aisle warily raised his hand.

"I'm Frank. And I lost my wife, Karen, several years ago." He stood to his feet, along with the woman next to him.

"I'm Karen's sister, Ann," said the woman.

I began to see Karen materialize next to Frank. She had long brown hair, and her skin appeared extremely soft. It gave me a sense of a peaches-and-cream complexion. Karen wore a long flowing white and pink gown. Interestingly enough, she pulled petals one by one from a white rose that she held and then let them cascade over her husband. Her thoughts were quite intense.

"Frank, your wife wants you to know that she sees you all the time and is with you all the time. She is mentioning a place called Moonshine. Do you know this?"

"Yes," he answered. He seemed surprised that I would know such things. "We met there."

"She is telling me that you used to go dancing there with friends."

"In college," he replied. "That's where we met. Wow, it's amazing!"

Frank was completely dumbfounded. I could tell he thought the whole experience a little surreal.

"She is telling me that you are and always have been a gentleman and is mentioning the name Crunch or the Cruncher. Do you understand this?"

Ann quickly placed her hand up to her mouth in recognition of what I had just said.

Frank continued, "Yes, the night I met her, there was this local guy named Cruncher. He was very wasted and was giving Karen a hard time. He was all over her, and I kind of stopped him."

I quickly added, "She is saying you did stop him!"

"Yeah. I crashed a beer bottle over his head, and the cops came and picked him up."

The crowd laughed.

"Karen now shows me that she is standing behind you while you sat in a white metal chair on the back deck."

"Yeah, I go there all the time. Gosh, this is unbelievable."

"She is waving her finger at you and saying, *You know better than that.*"

"I understand. I go out there every morning and every night and have a cigarette."

The audience aahed their recognition of his little secret.

"She is telling me that she can hear your thoughts, and she wipes away your tears."

Hearing this comment, Frank wept. "She was my life, my everything."

"Yes. And you are her everything!" I snapped back. "She is trying to help you to experience life once again, but is having a hard time because you don't want to budge. You are stuck on her memory and won't move on. There is no room in your heart for anyone or anything new in your life. She wants me to tell you that you gave her life."

"No, I didn't. I took it away. I should have been there for her. I should have had the medicine in the house when she needed it."

At this point Frank began to break down, and Ann began to rub his back to comfort him.

"She is telling me that one day you will meet another woman to love."

"I can never and will never love anyone else but Karen. My heart has been broken. When Karen died, she took my heart with her."

People in the audience moaned softly as they felt compassion for this man's heartbreak. At this point Frank had the same reaction I had seen hundreds of times before. When a departed partner tells the living one that he or she will fall in love again, the response is usually negative—"No, I will never love another!" But my job is to bring the message, not force anyone to believe it.

"Not all of it. Love has an unlimited supply," I replied. "She is saying you are afraid. You are living your life in complete fear."

Frank stared right through me. "I don't want to hurt anyone else."

At this point Karen's sister interrupted. "He doesn't even go out of the house. He hasn't been out of the house in over two years. It's crazy!"

Then Karen impressed me with another thought. "Do you know who Marcie is?"

Frank looked down at the floor. "Nah . . . I don't know who you are talking about."

"Was Karen ever unkind to Marcie? Because she is saying that it happened a long time ago. She shouldn't have behaved so badly. She wants to make it up to her. She feels she must do this."

"I don't know a Marcie."

Karen's sister whispered to Frank. "Isn't Marcie someone from college?" she asked. The two conversed a little and then looked back at me for more information.

"Karen wants you to go to the old Moonshine and have a dance for her. She promises you a good time."

"I don't go out anymore," said Frank.

"Karen is begging you to go for her sake. She is promising that it will change your life. She is being extremely insistent. She is telling me that you know that she is used to getting her way if it was something that she wanted."

"Watch out!" he shouted as he smiled. "Okay," he agreed, "I'll do it for Karen's sake."

After that, we ended the message.

Several months later, Kelley, my assistant, handed me a stack of mail. In the stack was an envelope that looked like an invitation. I opened it, and there was a note that read:

Dear James,

I wanted to thank you for giving me my life back. I never would have be-lieved it was possible if I hadn't experienced it myself that night. Weeks after contemplating my reading with you, I followed Karen's advice and went to the old Moonshine Club, where I ran into Marcie, an old college friend. The instant I saw her, I felt my chest pound. I had completely forgotten all about her until that moment. I know this was the same Marcie that Karen was telling us about. I am enclosing an invitation for our wedding and would like you to be a guest.

Regards,
Frank

I looked at the invitation that was in the shape of a heart. When I opened it up, it read:

My heart is made whole again.

Please join Marcie and Frank for a celebration

of an unlimited supply of LOVE.

Fear strikes people in different ways. Like Frank, we can become immobilized by fear. The energy of fear pulls us down to a place where life seems like a difficult task. Everything we do is clouded by fear's limitedness and discouragement. But we can't find what we really want behind a wall of fear. In Frank's case, he was unable to take a step out of fear and depression until he was surrounded by Karen's love. With the love of his wife in spirit, he was able to find even more love and happiness on earth.

FEAR NOT, MY LOVE

As the next reading shows, some have to wait until death in order to fully understand the negative impact of not only their lives, but also their beliefs on another's growth. I urge you, as you read on, to reflect on the ways fear may hinder you in your own life.

From the moment he could walk, Martin Katz was afraid. He was taught to be afraid by his mother and father. If he bumped into a table, they would quickly grab him for fear he would fall down and hit his head. They would keep him inside when it was snowing for fear he would get cold and wet and eventually, as his mother would constantly say, "catch his death." Most parents have a fair amount of concern for their children's safety, but Martin's parents took their concern to the extreme. Martin grew up with plenty of fears, especially the fear of death. In fact, fear became Martin's reality and ran his entire life.

Martin grew up in Brooklyn, New York, and lived in a small brownstone apartment. Every morning Martin's mother would walk him to school before she went to work, and every afternoon she would pick him up. If Martin didn't see his mother outside after school, he was forbidden to leave the school property until she showed up. One afternoon, Martin's mother didn't show up, and he waited several hours until she finally came to school. His mother said she was sorry but she had to work an extra shift that day. Because Martin was a fearful little boy, waiting for his mother seemed like an eternity. He thought about monsters coming to get him. Despite his obsessive fears, Martin managed to grow up pretty normally. He eventually married a wonderful woman named Charlotte and had two children.

I was doing a private reading for a small group when I had the opportunity to meet Martin. As I perused the group of nine people, there was one woman who stood out from the rest. She had long, stringy brown hair and oversized glasses. She kept fidgeting in her chair. Although it was common for people to be skittish when they come for a reading, this young woman seemed very high-strung.

I looked at her and asked, "Are you okay?"

"Yes, I think so. I have never done this before, so I am a little nervous."

I explained how communication worked, that I raised my energy and spirits lowered theirs, and somewhere in the middle we would meet. I also assured the group, "You have nothing to feel uncomfortable about." Then I lead a meditation so they could relax and release their nervous tension. It is difficult for me to work with excessive nervousness, because it blocks the flow of concentrated energy used in communication. By the time the meditation was over, everyone was calm, including the woman with the stringy hair, but I could still sense some discomfort around her.

Forty-five minutes and several messages later, I was ready to tackle the nervous woman in front of me.

"What is your name?"

"Stephanie."

I noticed a spirit pacing back and forth behind her. He was very on edge, just like her, and I wondered if she was picking up his anxiety. This is quite common. During my demonstrations, when spirits are agitated, people in the audience can sense their uneasy energy.

I telepathically told the spirit behind Stephanie, "Now is your time to speak. Now!"

I could sense his surprise. Then he thanked me.

"There is a man standing behind you. He is very nervous. He is giving me a name that sounds like Marty or Martin. Do you understand this?"

"Yes, that's my father, Martin. We called him Martin or Papa. But I don't understand. He didn't believe in life after death. He was totally afraid of things like this."

"He's sending you his love and wants you to know that he is no longer afraid of death. He says that he had it all wrong and feels so stupid for being fearful. He is saying that death is natural—it is painless."

As I relayed Martin's message to his daughter, he kept yelling at me to tell her, *I am here. I made it.*

Tears rolled down Stephanie's cheeks. Even though she had observed others in the group receive astounding messages, she was still in awe of the whole process.

"What was it like?" she queried.

"What do you mean?" I asked.

"His death. My father was so scared about death. What does he say?"

"He says that it was very natural. He remembers lying in the hospital bed watching television, and the next thing he knew, he saw his brother Max, who had died several years earlier. Then he saw his mother and father, and both of them looked so young. He was amazed that neither one had that worried look on their faces that he had seen all his life. He didn't quite understand where he was, and then Max told him to get up. Your father is saying that he was confused and told Max that he was sick and couldn't get out of bed. Max told him that he wasn't sick; it was all in his head. Max told him to just think about how good he would feel."

Martin had been sending me a lot of thoughts all at once. I knew I was talking fast just to keep up with him.

"Your father says that he got up, and suddenly he was in a beautiful garden surrounded by everyone he had ever met. He is telling me that it was the first time he felt free and not scared, not fearful. He says it felt like escaping from prison. Then his mother came to him and apologized for teaching him to be terrified of life."

Stephanie sat there in amazement as I conveyed her father's message.

"It's hard to believe it's really him," she said softly.

"Your father is telling me that fear damages you. It takes away your curiosity and your imagination to create. He wants me to tell you that anything is possible."

Then Martin told me something quite fantastic. "Do you understand law school?"

"Yes, I do. My father's dream was to be a lawyer. He wanted to seek justice for people and make a real change in their lives. But he never thought he was smart enough to be a lawyer. He became a salesman and sold shirts. He regretted the fact that he didn't even try to go to law school. He would often say to us that he wondered what would have happened if he wasn't so afraid."

"He is saying that he realizes he would have made a very good lawyer, if only he believed in himself. He is also telling me that he is going to get a second chance at his dream."

I did not understand what Martin meant by this remark and relayed that to Stephanie.

"I do." She began sobbing. "In two days I am scheduled to take the bar exam. Before I came here tonight, I was going to cancel out, because I was too afraid. I wasn't sure I could do it. I know differently now! I'm not afraid. Papa has given me hope."

"*And freedom*, he is telling me. *Because once and for all you love yourself enough to break the family chain of fear!*"

With that announcement, Martin threw his spirit arms around his daughter and gave her a kiss.

Like Martin's, our beliefs are formed by family upbringing, past experiences, and societal values. We view the world around us through these beliefs and measure ourselves, our worth, and our value in the world by what I call "old belief tapes." Because so many of the messages of those tapes are fear-based, we look at the world through fearful eyes, and we form our opinions and viewpoints from this distorted perspective. Fear blocks any recognition of our true selves. Because it is difficult to stay in the unnatural state of fear, feeling inadequate, insecure, unloved, misunderstood, angry, and sad, we turn to alcohol, drugs, food, gambling, sex, and whatever else to escape. We engage in these self-destructive behaviors to keep ourselves from feeling those unnatural, uncomfortable emotions.

One of the most fascinating studies of human interaction and behavior I have seen has been the television show *Intervention* on A&E. It is about families who come together to try to stop the self-destructive behavior of their loved ones. The only way they are able to succeed and get through to the addicted persons is through their combined power of love. The power of love is the strongest healing force imaginable.

Most people do not realize the effect their belief systems have on their everyday lives and the lives of others until it is too late or, as in Martin's case, until after they die. Often it takes a life-altering experience to make someone fully understand the consequences of fear. For some, this might be a terminal illness, an accident, a near-death experience, or perhaps a highly conscious moment of insight.

So many of us are driven by fear, and although it can certainly be a motivator to cause us to take action in life and do things we would not usually do, at the same time it lowers our vibrational energy. Besides, we tend to project our fears out in the world; like Martin's parents, we project them onto our children and others. In a vicious cycle, whatever we project out comes back to us.

A friend of mine once told me about an uncle who hated his job and yet stayed in it for twenty years, because he was so afraid of not finding another one. He thought he would become destitute. He looked for other jobs, but without much luck. No job seemed any better than the one he had, because he was unable to see opportunities through eyes clouded with fear. After twenty years in the same job, my friend's uncle had aged beyond his years and was severely depressed. He had grown rigid with tension and disheartened about life. He was not living; he was merely existing. His fear kept any good from coming his way, and he wound up with all that fear offered: hate, anger, resentment, and bitterness.

If we define our reality by measuring the world with our senses, our environment, and what we have been taught, we believe that only what we perceive around us is real. The truth is that life on earth is a temporary illusion. In fact, everything in the physical world is transitory. The only true constant is love—the power that creates and expands. Love knows no judgment or criticism; love just is.

It is the characteristics of love that draw people and situations to us. When we do something out of love, we create more love, but when we do something for the sake of money or fame, for instance, we may get those things, but our hearts and souls will be left empty. When we live with love, it affects us with positive characteristics such as joy, happiness, compassion, and laughter.

Take a few minutes and review some of the decisions and choices you made in your life. Were they from a place of love or fear? If you are happy and fulfilled, you are living in a loving space. However, if you feel unfulfilled, anxious, or insecure, you have let fear run your life, and you are living in the illusion of truth. From this moment on, become mindful of the decisions you make. If you make a decision and then worry about the outcome, you are coming from a place of fear, but if you do something that makes you happy, you are coming from love. With love, anything is possible, as you will see in this next reading.

LIFE'S ANGELS

It was during another one of my mediumship demonstrations that an incredible gift was given not only to the one intended, but also to all three hundred people in the room that night. Each person was touched by the words and experiences, the magical and healing insights of one particular spirit.

I was halfway through my demonstration when I noticed two spirits—a nurse and a doctor—behind a red-haired woman seated in the back of the room. The spirits were present for most of the night and were extremely patient in waiting their turn. Whenever I see medical spirits around someone, they are usually there for one of two reasons. Either these beings have come to aid in the healing of an individual with a health problem, or they are there to be guides and bring energy to someone who also works in the healing arts. In this case it was the latter.

"May I come to you, please?" I pointed at the red-haired woman.

"Yes, of course."

The nurse and doctor acknowledged me and blended slightly into the background. Another spirit, with honey blonde hair, red lips, and blue eyes appeared. She had an angelic smile. She also thanked me for letting her through.

"There is a lady standing next to you. Her name is Maureen. Do you know this person?"

"No, I don't recognize the name."

Then Maureen sent me another name. "Do you know Tibbett?"

"No. I have no idea who that is."

I could tell that this young woman was not aware of the name, because her mind was too fixated on who she wanted to hear from. That happens a lot in my work. People in the audience have certain loved ones in mind, not the spirits who actually do show up. Their fixation gets in the way, because their minds are not open to other possibilities. After a while (sometimes much later when they are on their way home) they finally remember the person trying to communicate with them. I guessed that this might be the case here. I could tell Maureen wanted to tell this woman something important, so she sent me another thought.

"Do you know the name Regency School?"

The woman's facial expression immediately changed when she made the connection. She burst into tears and was uncommunicative for several minutes. One of my assistants went to help her.

"Maureen is telling me she used to work at this school because of her love for children. She felt her mission on earth was to safeguard little children. That is why she is here tonight. Do you understand?"

The woman looked at me and said, "Yes, I understand. It's Maureen, the woman who saved my life."

At this point Maureen placed her hands on the woman's shoulders.

"Maureen is saying that she is your guardian angel."

"Maureen was a crossing guard at Regency School, where I went. She would always have a smile on her face and would give us gifts, sometimes a whistle or a lollipop. We loved her. The kids used to look forward to seeing Maureen or, as we called her, Mrs. Tibbett, because she was so pleasant and supportive. Kids would sit on her corner, and when she had time, she would play games with them. A lot of them felt more love from Mrs. Tibbett than from their own parents."

"She is telling me that she wanted to teach them what love was all about, so when they got older, they would know how to use it."

"I understand," the woman answered. "She gave me her ultimate love. I wish there was some way I could pay her back."

"For what?"

Through a stream of tears and occasional sobbing, this woman told the rest of her story.

"It was a Tuesday, and we had just gotten out of school. I was walking down the street when I saw my mother on the other side. I usually took the bus home, so I was surprised to see her. I was so excited that I ran across the street without looking. I heard a scream, and the next thing I knew I was lying in the gutter. There was a paramedic looking down at me, and my mother was holding my hand. I asked my mother what happened. She told me that when I ran across the street, a school bus had pulled away from the curb, and apparently the driver didn't see me in time. Mrs. Tibbett pushed me out of the way, so I was safe, but the bus crushed her, and she died. I have always wanted to thank her."

"Now is your moment," I enthusiastically replied.

With that comment, the woman looked up toward the ceiling and let out a loud, "Thank you, Maureen."

Everyone in the room was moved.

"Maureen is saying, *No reason to thank me, dear one. You have made me proud. Not only do you demonstrate love, but you too have saved lives.*"

When I transmitted Maureen's words to the red-haired woman, she humbly said, "No, I am nothing like Mrs. Tibbett."

"What did she mean by saving lives?" I asked, curious to understand the correlation between these two women.

She smiled. "I am a critical-care nurse for premature babies."

In closing, I turned to the audience and said, "Love! It's the gift of life."

Love has no boundaries. It is not possessive or jealous, nor is it based on conditions. There are no strings attached to love. As you have witnessed from the readings here, love does not hold back. If we all decided to live in love instead of fear, there would be no blame, no war, and no hurt. As we are made in the likeness of God, and God is Love, then we must strive to express our love in everything we do, say, and are.

PART TWO

do unto
OTHERS

FOUR

The Blame Game

Take your life in your own hands and what happens?
A terrible thing: no one to blame.

—Erica Jong

It is unfortunate that so many people cannot find it in their hearts to be more loving. Because they cannot, conflict exists. It occurs between family members, friends, organizations, communities, and even governments. We would rather blame someone else for our mistakes and problems than take responsibility for our actions. The blame game seems to be a normal part of life: if I am right, then you must be wrong. It's much easier to blame than to make an attempt to understand others through love and forgiveness.

We learn blaming behavior at an early age. For instance, if a child does something she knows is wrong and is caught, she tends to place the blame on another child. She doesn't want to suffer the consequences her mother may dish out for the wrongdoing. If a child gets away with this behavior often enough, she will become programmed that it's okay to blame others if it will keep her from being punished.

I have met so many people who need—and want—to place blame on others for their life circumstances, because it is so much easier to make someone else responsible for their disappointments and unrealized dreams. People don't want to admit that they made wrong choices. If they continue to go through life with this mind-set, they will fall into *victim consciousness*. Victim consciousness, or what I like to call the "pity party," seems normal for many. Essentially, like the child who doesn't want to be punished, we don't want to take responsibility if something goes wrong. Therefore, we end up becoming victims of our circumstances and blaming something other than ourselves for the mess we are in.

YOU DIDN'T LOVE ME ENOUGH

The following reading is about victim consciousness. The woman involved blamed her parents for the person she had become and the circumstances in which she found herself.

Adrienne Zeil came to a women's conference I took part in in Desert Hot Springs, California, in 2005. There were a total of forty women, from a variety of economic, social, and political backgrounds, who came from all over the country. Some were struggling with grief, others wanted spiritual enlightenment, and still others were just plain curious.

As I looked around at the women seated before me, I received an impression of a 1967 Impala, and I explained what I was seeing to the audience.

"This car is on its way up a mountain road heading for a cabin. It's having a hard time getting around the curves and hills. In fact, it is stopping on the side of the road occasionally to take a break.

The women laughed at this scenario.

Suddenly, a petite woman spoke up. "Yes, I understand that picture."

The small woman with black curly hair wore wire-rimmed glasses.

She sat in the second row. "My father had an Impala, and he would often drive it to our mountain cabin."

I walked over to her. "What is your name?"

"Adrienne. But you can call me Addie."

"Thanks for acknowledging this message," I said.

"Is my dad here? I have been waiting to talk to him for a long time. We never said good-bye to each other."

With that comment, I received an impression of a name. "Would you know the name Nathan or Nat?"

"Yes, that's his name."

"And would you know the name Joan?"

"Yes, that's my mother."

I could tell all of the women were impressed and at the same time a bit unnerved.

"Do you know about Jackson sitting in the backseat?"

"Yes, Jackson is my brother. He sat next to me every trip. We always fought in the car, and my parents always blamed me for starting the fights," Adrienne said with a nervous laugh.

"Your father wants me to tell you that he loves you, and your mother is standing by his side smiling."

"Oh, I don't think so," she abruptly responded. "My father never knew the meaning of the word."

I looked at her father's face, and he was smiling. In fact, he was beaming with compassion.

"He is saying that he could have said it more to you. He says that when he was in our world, he did not love himself enough, so he didn't feel comfortable telling others he loved them. Your mother is nodding her head. She says she felt the way you did about your father."

Adrienne did not quite understand. "I never knew this about my mother," she said. "She never mentioned it."

Then her mother spoke. "Your mother is telling me that they tried giving you the best life they could, but you refused to accept it."

"That's not true! They gave me nothing. They were always telling me how I wasn't good enough. They never encouraged me. It was always about Jackson. He was the oldest, so he got all the attention. I never asked for much. I just wanted supportive parents. Things could have been so much better for me if I felt their love and approval. Can I just ask them why? Why didn't they encourage me?"

Suddenly, Joan filled my head up with some amazing memories of her daughter. "Addie, do you remember the ice-skating contest?"

Adrienne looked down.

"Do you remember what your mother said to you?"

"Yeah. I was going to quit, because I didn't think I was good enough."

"What did she tell you?"

"She told me to close my eyes and see myself as the winner, and skate like that."

"And?" I asked.

"I did. And I won the contest. God, I haven't remembered that in years."

Then her father filled me with another memory. "Did you win a scholarship for school?"

"Oh my God. I can't believe it. Yes, a partial one."

"Your father is mentioning a graduation reward."

Adrienne was smiling.

"What did your father do?"

She thought about it for a moment. Then it seemed a lightbulb went off in her mind. "I know what he is trying to say. He told me that he would pay the remainder of the tuition for the four years, if I would go through with it."

"And what did you do?" I asked.

"I thought it was just another way he could have control over me, so I didn't agree to his offer. I took his money, but I spent it on an apartment in the city to study art, which, unfortunately, I was never good at."

"Your mother is saying that you were a wonderful artist, Addie. She says you did something for her on Mother's Day."

Adrienne shook her head and sighed. "I did a portrait of her. It was actually pretty good. In fact, I sold it. It was the first and last piece of art I ever sold."

These several reminders caused Adrienne to do a quick review of her life and see where her sense of blame originated. She stared at me.

"I didn't believe in my own possibilities. I found more power in being the victim. I would say how awful everyone else was, so I didn't have to look at how I didn't want to take responsibility for myself."

"Well, Addie, your parents want to thank you for your love."

"How could they? I am so ashamed and so sorry for blaming them for everything."

"No. They want to thank you for helping them to help you."

"Huh? What are you talking about?"

"By how you limit yourself and don't believe in yourself—your parents get an extra opportunity in spirit to help you. They can assist and influence you in finding the light in your own heart that you have kept hidden for so long. It seems they were not able to or didn't know how to get through to you when they were alive, but now it is easier to motivate you. They say you seem much more open to them, so they can be with you and help you to remember your spiritual power."

Adrienne was dumbfounded by this last comment.

I continued, "Your parents are melding their thoughts together and saying you have already begun to find your power. They helped to create a situation for you last week, and you did it! They are very proud of you."

"I'm not sure what that means."

"Did you sign up for an art class last week?"

"Yes, as a matter of fact, I did. I was walking down a street that I never go down, and there in an art supply store window was an advertisement for an art class. I don't know what came over me, but I went in and signed up. It just felt right."

"Joan and Nat set that up. They want me to tell you one more thing."

"What is that?"

"You are never too old to learn how great you are, and they will always be by your side."

"Thank you, James." Then Adrienne looked up and said, "I love you, Mom and Dad."

"By the way, your dad wants to thank you for the Impala. I am not sure what that means."

"Oh, last year I went online to see if I could find my dad's old car, and I traced it to a place in New Mexico. I bought it back and have it in my garage."

With that comment, everyone in the room applauded.

When I first met Adrienne, she was combative and angry. It was amazing to see that by the end of the reading, she seemed lighter. Adrienne's parents gave her one of the greatest gifts of healing. Through their communication, they helped Adrienne look at herself with a new perspective for the very first time. The result was that she took the necessary steps to emancipate herself from the self-imposed prison in her mind.

We are on this earth to learn many lessons, but the most important lesson is to love and accept ourselves for who we are. There is always the internal struggle of trying to fit in and be acceptable in the eyes of others. When we judge others and ourselves, we are not seeing the truth, for judgment equals fear. By playing the blame game and living in victim consciousness, we perpetuate and project fear, because the mind-set of a victim is one of fear. When we look through the eyes of fear, we immediately get caught up in illusion and limitation: "I'm not good enough. I'm not meant to succeed in life." These are lies against our divine nature.

Victims make choices from a distorted view. They attract slightly *off* experiences to themselves and are caught in the endless, vicious cycle of this self-wounding mentality. Usually victims act like victims in every aspect of their lives. If they feel they have no power, how can things ever be different?

Many of you have been around people whose attitude is self-defeating and depressing. These people are not very popular, because their negative attitude pushes others away. At the same time, they tend to draw into their lives other like-minded victims who have the same fearful mentality. You know the expression: misery loves company. How can anyone succeed in life when surrounded by negative energy? With such a dismal outlook on life, victims always feel as though they have been dealt a bad hand.

I honestly believe that many societal problems come from this victim mentality. In many ways, depression, anger, insecurity, distrust, and violence stem from this type of thinking. Yes, it is true that many live in underprivileged conditions and are denied the information and education available to others in more privileged circumstances. However, if individuals, despite their situations, do not seek a world past the one they know and attempt to learn the skills to understand and become aware of their true selves, they will continue to live in these adverse and restricted conditions. Because so many are locked into familiarity— "It's all I know"—they are reluctant to go beyond their comfort level and take risks. They limit themselves because of their very narrow view. Unfortunately, when people continually deny responsibility for their choices, they take on a "them against me" mentality. *They* are keeping *me* from a better job, a better salary, a better home, and so forth. On a national level, a them-against-me mind-set is a prescription for war.

When we think with a them-against-me mentality, we narrow our understanding of the world's diversity. This mentality quickly fosters prejudice. Prejudice means not having all the facts and making choices based on incomplete information.

I am often asked, "If a loved one passes into spirit, does he or she magically possess complete awareness and knowledge of the entire Universe?" My answer is, "No, not really." Yes, spirits do have a more expansive perspective on life and death. However, if they were locked into a particular mind-set on earth, especially victim consciousness or a blame-game mentality, they will not shake it off so easily, even after entering the light. Unfortunately, the negative emotions attached to this mind-set will still be intact.

IT'S ALL THEIR FAULT

I would like to share with you a message that came through during an event in Detroit, Michigan. I hope you will appreciate the profound value of having an open mind.

During this particular workshop, I commented to one of my assistants that the energy of the room was wonderful. The people seemed so receptive and willing to question their perceptions and feelings. I had finished three emotional readings, and the audience was eager for what was to come. So to say that I was shocked and stunned at the next spirit message is an understatement.

Since the beginning of the evening, I had noticed a female spirit, wearing a white and gray housedress covered by an apron, hanging around a young woman in the audience. This spirit stood around in her white-stockinged feet. She held what seemed to be a Bible or prayer book in her hand. Most of the time, her head was bowed as if she was reading from it. From time to time, she would look up at me. After turning a page in her book, she finally communicated to me by pointing her finger and telepathically asking, *Who are you? I want to talk to my granddaughter.*

I mentally inquired what her name was.

Sophie, she replied.

I looked around the area where the spirit was standing and asked,

"Does someone over here have a grandmother by the name of Sophie? She is saying she lived in a place that sounds like Otter or Otterville."

Immediately, the young woman rose to her feet. "I do. My grandmother's name is Sophie! And she lived in Otterville, Ohio. Is she here?"

"Oh, she's here, all right."

The woman seemed surprised that her granddaughter stood up so quickly. Then she yelled at me, *You're the devil! You're going to go to hell!*

"Your grandmother, Sophie, thinks that what I am doing is wrong. Was she a very religious woman?"

"Oh, yes. She was a die-hard Baptist and thought anyone who didn't believe her way would burn in hell."

At this remark, Sophie pointed to her prayer book.

The young woman then asked, "Is there hell? Can she tell me?"

"She is saying that she would not know, because she has accepted Jesus as her savior."

"Has she seen Jesus?"

"No. But she is telling me that one of his followers is taking care of her. *This is his heaven,* she says. *Those who don't know him go somewhere else.*"

"Oh!" The granddaughter seemed somewhat embarrassed by her grandmother's attitude.

"What's your name, please?" I asked the young woman.

"Celeste."

"Well, Celeste, your grandmother is giving me the sense that hers was the only rightful religion."

Then Sophie interrupted me. *I am here because I am happy to be out of it all. I want my grandbaby to know that. I was sick and tired of being taken advantage of.*

"Your grandmother is saying that your father was an all-right man, but that he should have taken better care of his family. He was a bit of a loafer. He should have provided more, especially because of his background."

I turned to Celeste, "Does this make any sense to you?"

"Yes, it does. Grandma never liked my father because he was Jewish. She was against my mother marrying him, and they never got along because of that."

Then Sophie exploded loudly in my head. *He was a Jew and those people belong with their own. It's because of them Jews that everything changed.*

As the spirit got angrier and louder, I put my hands up to my ears. I repeated what she said to Celeste.

"Sophie is very angry. She says that they came into the town and took over everything. Banks, stores, you name it. They took her father's house away during the Depression."

I could hear murmuring in the audience, but I had to keep up with the spirit's message.

"Your grandmother has a lot of prejudice in her heart. Did she always blame others for the conditions in her life?"

"She always blamed someone for something, and especially the Jews. She was not a happy person. We were actually thankful when she finally passed. I am sorry to say it, but it was a relief."

It was obvious that Sophie still had a lot to learn. I sent her a thought of compassion and love.

Celeste asked, "Are you happy, Grandma?"

"Your grandmother says, *I guess I am.* She says that she never knew how uncomfortable she made you feel. She's sorry."

Celeste smiled.

Then I relayed Sophie's comments to the audience. *It is beautiful here, very beautiful. This place makes me feel good. You know it's the first time in my life people treated me so nicely, or at least I feel that way. Heaven is nothing like I expected. There is a nice, tall gentleman who helps me.*

"Who is it?" asked Celeste.

"Your grandmother says she doesn't know, but that he's been with her ever since she arrived. Her words are, *I have never met such a caring individual. He must be an angel sent from Jesus.* She says that this angel shows her things—things she would never have understood on her own. That is why she ventured here tonight. Otherwise, she would think that this is the devil at work."

The audience grew quiet as they listened closely to what Sophie had to say.

"Sophie is telling me that her angel thought it would be good for her to feel the love in this room. She also wanted to let her grandbaby know that there is nothing to be scared of when she passes over. She says that since she started to speak to me, the room has become more beautiful. It has a glow about it."

"Who is this angel?" Celeste inquired.

"She thinks he's a helper of sorts. He helps people adjust to life there. Your grandmother is saying that she has to go now, because other people have to come in. She wants you to take care of yourself. She is very proud of you."

At that point, Celeste beamed.

I saw Sophie turn around and walk toward a tall gentleman in the distance. By his energy, I knew that this angel was an evolved being and one of Sophie's guides. I could see him smile at Sophie as if to say, "Well done." As they turned to leave, I recognized a yarmulke on the guide's head and tallis around his shoulders. How ironic, I thought. Sophie's guide appeared to be a rabbi.

Sophie was a true victim of life. It was easier for her to blame a particular group of people, or "them," for her unhappiness. It was easier for her to blame than to change what she didn't like in her life. By falling into this mind trap, she took the easy way out. Blaming others became an automatic bad habit.

Until we rise up and take responsibility for our thoughts, we will be stuck in this blame-game mentality. Life is not always pleasant; in fact, it can be very painful. Sometimes you have to choose between something bad and something even worse, but these choices teach you and you grow. Whatever the outcome, you have created it. Therefore, *you,* and *only you,* become the author of your destiny. When you take a personal interest in every choice you make and every step you take on this path of life, you will feel more confident and unafraid.

We all want the easy way out, but if we take the easy way out, we shut ourselves off from growing, learning, and understanding. By taking responsibility, we give ourselves a place in the world; we measure how we perceive ourselves, each other, and the world at large. Individuals who take responsibility attract other responsible human beings into their lives.

Ultimately, it is your thoughts that color the atmosphere around you. No one can *make* you feel anything. You have to be *willing* to feel a certain way. Only you can allow others' thoughts into your head. You must take responsibility for your actions. How does your action affect the life of another? Those who are angry and blameful find that their actions mirror how they feel. If they feel insecure, they create upheaval not only inside themselves, but in others as well.

I BLAME MYSELF

The following reading demonstrates exactly what I mean about taking responsibility for our thoughts and behavior, and finding peace within ourselves even after we think that we made the wrong decision. It also demonstrates the ultimate price we pay for not being true to ourselves.

I was in New York at my annual workshop and had spent about twenty minutes playing referee between the two Salerno brothers. Louis, the deceased, blamed his fifty-five-year-old living brother, Anthony, who was in the audience, for undermining their restaurant business.

"Louis says, *Tony, you were never responsible for anything. You always borrowed money and promised to pay it back. You made the business go belly-up. Did I ever see a nickel?*"

The way Louis spoke to his brother brought back memories of

growing up in New York and visiting the downtown section of Little Italy. Images of slices of pizza and lemon ices filled my mind as Anthony looked at the ceiling and responded.

"Are you kiddin' me or what?" Anthony retorted. "You always took money for the girls. You had to wine and dine them on everything. The money went to them."

Then I became aware of a young man's spirit. He seemed to be about twenty-one, wore a buzz cut, and stood next to Anthony. He sent me his thoughts.

I asked Anthony, "Do you know about *scramble*? There is a young, brown-haired man here mentioning the word *scramble*. Do you understand?"

"No, I don't know what you're talking about."

I asked the spirit to send me more information. Suddenly two other young men came forward and stood by Anthony's left side. They melded their thoughts together and fed them to me. *Eagle Squadron. We're from Eagle Squadron.*

Once again I asked Anthony, "Do you know Eagle Squadron?"

Once again he answered, "No, I don't have a clue."

I often think of myself as an air-traffic controller when I communicate between the spirit and physical worlds. I may be working with one person when another spirit cuts in. It takes me a while to figure out that the new spirit does not belong to the person to whom I am speaking. This seemed to be the case with Anthony.

"I am sorry, Anthony, but your brother's energy has faded, and I am aware now of several young men coming to me and telling me that they fought together with someone in this audience."

I quickly scanned the room and noticed that several people were quite amazed by my quick change of images. "Is there anyone else in the room who can make sense of this?"

One young guy sitting at the end of Anthony's row rubbed his hands together and mumbled, "I might."

The woman sitting next to him immediately grabbed his hand and whispered something in his ear. Then I saw a spirit woman standing directly behind this woman. She had red hair and her face was fully made up as though she were going to a dance. I knew instantly that this spirit was the woman's deceased mother and the young man's grandmother.

"Ma'am, there is a woman standing behind you. She is all dolled up and wearing a yellow dress."

"Oh, that sounds like my mother. She wouldn't go anywhere without her face on."

The spirit wanted to give a message to her grandson.

"She is saying *Jason.* Does that name refer to anyone?"

"Yes," said the young man. "That's my name."

"Your grandma wants you to know that she is here to bring you love and strength, and she always will."

"Thanks," Jason responded.

Then the spirit woman said, *Tell him about the photograph.*

"She wants me to tell you that she is aware of the photograph of her you keep in your wallet."

Jason was taken aback by this message. "Yes . . . that's right. I always keep it with me." His eyes glistened with tears.

"Were you in the Marines? She is showing me a vision of a tank, and you are in uniform. I see her picture with you."

I could sense that this information seemed to make Jason a bit uncomfortable. He gazed down at the ground. His mother ran her hand through his hair and mouthed that it was all right.

After a few seconds, Jason looked at me and said, "Yes. I was in the Second Marine Expeditionary Brigade. I was a gunner."

I nodded to him. "Your grandmother was with you. She said you used to put her picture on top of the tank window."

"Yes, she's right. I stuck it on there with gum."

As he spoke, the three spirit guys from before appeared next to the grandmother. Each one had an expression of compassion on his face.

Suddenly, Jason's grandmother pleaded, *Please, please tell him he is for-given. He needs to forgive himself. No one is angry with him. In my world, all is seen as okay. We don't judge the same as you do in your world. I beg you to tell him not to do this to himself.* She was saying that the whole thing was an accident.

As I conveyed the message, Jason cried softly, putting his palms to his eyes to hide his tears. He made strange, unintelligible sounds.

One of the male spirits spoke to me.

"Do you know Keith? Or Johnny Q? Or Benson? I am being given these names."

Jason quickly raised his head. "Yes, I do! They were pilots from the Eagle Squadron on a recon mission."

Suddenly, Jason stood up and yelled, "It wasn't my fault! I told Clark not to attack. No one was sure. It wasn't my fault. Leave me alone!"

The disturbed young man ran out of the room quickly, followed by his mother. The three spirit men and the grandmother drifted off.

I was dumbfounded; the rest of the audience became absolutely silent. It was as if a train had come to an unexpected halt; no one knew what to do.

Feeling drained, I sat down in my chair and then looked at the crowd. "I think it's time we close for the evening." I recited a short prayer, mentioning Jason to make sure everyone kept him in their thoughts.

After most events, I stay to sign books and take photographs with the workshop participants. Even though I was exhausted and wanted to leave, I stayed anyway. Several people waited to have their books signed and to meet me. Many people seemed to still be stunned by the last reading. As I reached to sign the next book, I noticed that the man standing before me was Anthony Salerno.

In his Soprano-type accent, he asked, "So, that's it? My brother just left?"

"I'm sorry, Anthony, but I have closed down for the evening. Sorry."

"No, that's all right." He reached into his pocket and pulled out a business card and handed it to me. I noticed that he was president of his own stationery supply company.

"If Louis comes back again, can you call me?"

"Well, I don't think he will, Anthony. You have a better chance of seeing him than I do. After all, he's your brother."

"Okay. What about that kid? Do you think you'll ever find out about that kid who ran out? You know, I was in the Marines a long time ago, so I know what guys like him go through. If you hear from him, and he needs anything, give me a call."

"Thank you, Anthony. That's kind of you."

Several months later, I received a card in the mail:

Dear James,

My son Jason and I were at the September New York event. You may re-member us, because my son ran out of the room feeling very upset. Ever since that time, Jason has gotten worse. He has dreamed of the three dead pilots you had mentioned in your reading. Unfortunately, Jason began taking pain pills and antidepressants. I came home from work one day and found him on the bed. He was dead. Next to him was a suicide note. I made a copy for you. I learned that Jason was part of a mission that accidentally killed three soldiers in friendly fire. He was so distraught and could not forgive himself. I have often blamed myself for bringing him to your event, but he had been depressed for a long time. I know it is not your fault, James, for what my son has done, but I did want you to know what had happened to him.

Sincerely,
Sherry Troy

I was shocked and upset. I picked up the copy of the suicide note. It read:

Mom,

I can no longer go on knowing I have killed my brothers. Not being man enough to take the responsibility, I blamed their deaths on someone else. I am sorry I could not be all I was supposed to be. I love you.

Jason

I sat there for a while feeling somewhat devastated. Then I remembered the card that Anthony had handed me. I immediately went into my box of business cards and found Anthony's phone number. I called him and explained what had happened.

A year or so later, I ran into Anthony at another event. "Hey, James, remember my brother, Louis, and the Marine you called me about?"

"Yes, of course, Anthony."

"Well, my brother, Louis, was right. The money he said I took, I did. I put it away, you know, for a rainy day. Anyway, after you called me about that young kid, I wanted to do something. Poor kid, he was so confused like so many other soldiers. So I took that money I saved and started an organization for vets with post-traumatic stress syndrome."

I was completely stunned. "I am so proud of you, Anthony. Good for you."

"I knew you would say that. I bet it made Louis happy."

"And I am sure he's not the only one."

Jason was overwrought with self-blame and spiraled down into a very dark place. We could all learn a lesson from him and that is this. *You* and *only you* have the power to move your life forward. You don't have to feel like a victim of life's circumstances. Jason had no control over the events of war. Whatever he blamed himself for created a very deep wound in his soul. I urge you to stop blaming yourself, the people who raised you, your teachers, your boss, or a particular segment of society for the problems in your life. Instead, keep a healthy mind-set. This is the only way to bring yourself up from the depths to a joyful level.

Many of us have a difficult time forgiving ourselves for past mistakes. Forgiveness plays an important role in letting go of blame and victimization. If Jason had realized that he was a small part of a much bigger picture, and that his buddies' deaths were necessary and natural for their souls' ultimate growth, perhaps he would still be alive today. Jason had to forgive himself, but it must have been too difficult a lesson for him to learn. His soul will bring this lesson again to him in another life.

Forgive and Forget

Forgiveness is not an occasional act;
it is a permanent attitude.

—Martin Luther King, Jr.

Besides love, forgiveness is the most powerful spiritual tool we possess. We can indeed change our destiny, the world, and ourselves by choosing to forgive. When someone is hurt, that hurt, left to fester, can grow into resentment. Time after time I have watched untreated resentment grow like weeds and ravage a person, choking off all life in its path. I have seen loving, fun-filled friendships turn into sources of bitterness and hate because neither side was able to forgive.

So, what is forgiveness? Forgiveness is a gift we give ourselves. It is a conscious choice to not get caught up in resentment or thoughts of revenge against another. We energetically unbind ourselves from thoughts and feelings that attach us to the offense. By choosing to forgive, we do not minimize the responsibility of the offender or justify the wrong. Rather, we free ourselves of our own negative thoughts.

Without a doubt, humans are creatures of habit. We love to hold on to things; we are not necessarily eager to change. The people who tend to hurt us are those closest to us—our partners, friends, family members, and co-workers. We love and place a fair amount of trust in these individuals, thinking it is okay to be vulnerable with them. We trust that they would never hurt us. In a way we set ourselves up for hurt. We expect them to be a certain way and don't like it when they are themselves and not like we expect. Many times we project our own ideals onto our friends and family—ideals they can never attain. So when things do not go as planned, and we feel hurt, betrayed, rejected, or insulted, we can find it extremely difficult to forgive.

Many of us believe that if we forgive someone who has wronged or hurt us, somehow we have given in and been defeated. We feel that if we forgive the wrongdoer, this will give the person permission to hurt us again. At the same time, by not forgiving the wrongdoer, we seem to have some sense of self-justification and power over the other person— a "You are wrong, I am right" sort of thing. We want to teach the person a lesson. However, when it comes right down to it, holding on to grudges sets us up for even more false expectations. We hope that our actions will cause the person to be sorry and not act that way again. Unfortunately, this usually doesn't work, and even if it did, the spiritual lesson has yet to be learned. If we want a relationship or situation to change, we have to be willing to express what we want. If the person does not want to change, then we must accept that fact and move on.

Another reason we don't forgive is because it is natural to fall into survival mode. Our egos feel instinctively better being angry with someone, because when we are angry, our egos are in control of the situation. When we stay angry with the other person, we are definitely in charge.

The three major emotional centers of the body are the lower stomach, the solar plexus, and the heart. When we don't forgive, our grudges become lodged in one or more of these energy centers. When I work clairvoyantly with others, I clearly see their energy centers and whether their energy is flowing up and through their bodies as it should. It is like watching water flowing. I can tune into a person's energy flow and observe any blocks that impede the flow. I cannot tell you the count-less times I have witnessed brown, patchy blotches in the stomach area or pockets of gray around the heart. If these emotional blocks remain indefinitely, they very well might manifest themselves as physical ail-ments or disease.

So if forgiveness can have such a dramatic effect on our minds and bodies, why is it that we find it so difficult to forgive ourselves and others? When we die, we carry the overwhelming effect of lack of forgiveness with us and have to live with it on the other side, where we may become mentally obsessed with not having resolved the situation while on earth. At the same time, the person on earth can feel this lingering tug of not having been forgiven.

THE TWINS

We never know in life why we find ourselves in certain families or in the different situations that present themselves to us. But when we start to look at life from a spiritual perspective, we realize that we have been put together with others in certain circumstances we have chosen to experience before we were born into this incarnation. The following reading describes how two souls from a past life chose to come back, this time to teach a soul lesson to one another about the astounding power of forgiveness.

"May I come to you?" I asked, as I pointed to a blonde woman who appeared to be in her late fifties.

Her response was similar to that of many of my audience members. She looked on either side of her, then looked back at me and pointed to herself.

"Do you mean me?" she asked in a surprised tone.

"Yes, you!" I replied. "There are two women standing behind you. One is a thin older woman, smoking a cigarette. She is thanking you for bringing her cigarettes. Do you understand?"

"Oh my God. That's my Aunt Rita. I used to sneak her cigarettes when she was in the hospital. She had emphysema."

"Well, that wasn't too smart!" I joked.

"Oh, well, she was on her way out anyway. I wanted to do anything that would make her happy."

The audience laughed.

I smiled and continued, "She is quite the personality. She is telling me that she helped to raise you. You were like a daughter to her."

This remark took the woman by surprise.

"What is your name, please?"

She answered, "My name is Becky."

At this point, I thought my eyes were playing tricks on me. Standing directly behind Becky, next to Aunt Rita, was another woman who looked like an identical younger version of Becky. Right away, I could tell by this spirit's energy that she had passed with a cancerous condition. Aunt Rita seemed to be encouraging a reunion of some sort between these two women.

"Becky, did you have a twin sister who passed with cancer?"

Instantly, Becky's whole demeanor changed. She seemed to have shut down, as if she had crawled into a hole.

"Yes. I had a sister, Pam, who died of breast cancer about five years ago."

I could see the spirit's energy light up with Becky's acknowledgment of her. Then Becky's twin began to transmit thoughts and feelings to me to share with her sister.

"Pam is sending me thoughts of regret. She is very sorry about what happened between the two of you. She is asking for your forgiveness."

Becky responded, "Whatever!" And as she said it, she swept her hand in front of her face in a gesture of dismissal.

I could tell that it was not going to be easy for Becky to listen to Pam's plea.

"She is saying she should have known better. She should have called you. She should have helped you with money. So many years were wasted."

Tears welled up in the older woman's eyes. She pulled a tissue from her purse. "It's too late. My sister was dead to me ten years ago. She left me with nothing. She stole my mother's things. She was a crook!"

I could see that Becky had been holding on to her hurt for many years, but it felt like the tip of an iceberg—something ran very deep between these two women. But first she had to resolve the present problem.

"She really needs you to forgive her. Not only for her sake, but yours. This anger you have is beginning to affect you," I said. I could see a dark gray blockage above her stomach. "Have you had a problem in the past several months in regard to digestion?"

Becky just shook her head up and down in validation.

Pam's spirit sent me an overpowering blend of celestial thoughts and impressions of what she had been going through since she had returned to the spirit world. I attempted to describe these impressions as quickly as she fed them to my mind.

"Pam's passing into spirit seemed very natural and very real to her. In some ways things are much easier there, and in some ways not. She had to see herself honestly, as everyone does when they enter that realm. Everyone sees others for who they are. You two appear as twins, but you are extremely different."

"Yes, that's right."

"Your sister is telling me that, because you both had such a deep love and strong soul connection in previous lifetimes, you chose to come back this time to work out your karmic obligations and share your soul lessons. You came to understand the nature of each other's personality and learn the desires and needs of the other. In many ways you were opposite. Yet, like two halves of a whole, you had to complete one another."

Now a new thought entered my mind. "Have you ever been to South Africa?"

Becky seemed perplexed with this question, but also quite curious.

"It is so weird that you should say that. Ever since my sister and I learned geography, all we wanted to do was visit South Africa. We used to beg our father all the time. That is so weird."

"Your sister wants you to know that in another life you belonged to a family who mined diamonds in Johannesburg. You were quite wealthy."

"Oh my God!" replied Becky. "I can't believe it."

Then Pam gave me a visual of a diamond.

"Was there an issue in this lifetime regarding a diamond or diamonds that she didn't share with you?"

By the reaction on Becky's face and also on the face of the woman next to her, I thought they both were going to faint.

"Oh . . . gosh, yes. This is amazing. She stole my mother's diamond bracelet, among other things."

"She is extremely sorry and wants you to forgive her. She says, *They are just things*. She wants you to understand the motivation behind it, and your shared history in a previous life."

"What do you mean?"

"In that lifetime in Johannesburg, you were the father, and she was one of your many daughters. Out of all the daughters she was your favorite. You would bring her to the mines when you went for the diamonds. At the end of every day, you would put a small diamond in a pouch to save for her. You promised that when she grew up, you would make a beautiful bracelet for her, fit for a queen. But, instead, she woke up one morning and you, the diamonds, and all the family belongings were gone. The rest of her life was spent in search of you, her father, but she never found you. She died impoverished and unloved. When you two came back as twins, you made a pact never to leave each other again."

This dialogue seemed too much for Becky. After a long sigh, she admitted, "I spent my whole life wanting to be with Pam. We were so close. Yet one day she took off, and I was very angry. Then, on top of that I found out that she stole my mother's diamond bracelet."

I asked Becky to look at the situation from a higher, spiritual perspective. "You both were supposed to learn about sharing and forgiveness. You repeated what happened in the South African lifetime. Now you will have to repeat the lesson again."

Becky was astounded by my explanation. "I feel so bad. I am sorry, Pam. Can you forgive me?"

"She already has," I commented. "She loves you very much. She asks that you remember to call her son, Michael.

"Really? Will he speak to me?"

"She is saying yes. She has visited Michael in his dreams and told him to find you. She wants you to have her red shoes that are still in her closet. Inside those red shoes you will find the bracelet."

Everyone in the audience, myself included, was amazed by this communication. I was overwhelmed by the amount of love that transcended death and, more than death, lifetimes. Becky's tear-filled eyes looked at me as if she had just discovered a new life. And she did.

Many times when I work with spirits, one comes through to tell a loved one in the audience to forgive those in life who have hurt him or her. This is done for a very good reason. Becky's years of resentment took their toll on her emotional, mental, and physical health. Her digestive system was in turmoil, and she was emotionally stressed and strained. When we give enough power to these negative emotions, they rear their ugly heads in ways that are unhealthy and, in some cases, even life-threatening. The most important part of forgiveness is letting go of the negative qualities associated with the situation or the person and bringing in the love. Love is the supreme healing force on the planet. Forgiveness and love go hand in hand, as you will see from the following incident.

THE GREATEST GIFT

When I first moved to Los Angeles, I worked as a clerical floater at Midway Hospital. Since I never had a desire to work in a hospital, I wondered why I took such a job and, even more, why I stayed on permanently. Looking back, I can understand that the hospital job afforded me many lessons. As you will understand from the following scenario, I learned probably one of the richest lessons of my life there. This particular lesson in forgiveness was one that gave me immense joy.

Wednesdays in the hospital usually meant working in the record-keeping department to organize the files. It was a bit monotonous. However, I looked forward to the afternoons, when at two o'clock a particular volunteer would show up. The volunteers at Midway Hospital (and all hospital volunteers in general) were and are amazing. This particular group of resilient senior citizens ran the guest-services desk and the gift shop, helped in the administration office, and did whatever odd jobs were necessary to assist the hospital staff. Because the hospital was located in a predominantly Jewish area of town known as the Fairfax district, most of the volunteers were Jewish. During my stint in the hospital, I became close to many of the volunteers, and one especially. His name was Art. Art would show up on Wednesday afternoons and help me for hours sticking labels onto file folders. We always had lively discussions about life. Our time together went on for months.

Then one November afternoon, Art didn't show up at his usual time. When he didn't show up the following Wednesday afternoon, I asked my supervisor, "Do you know where Art is?"

She replied, "Didn't you hear? He was admitted to the hospital as a patient. He's on the third floor."

During my break, I made my way up to the third floor in search of Art. I walked down the hall until I found him in room 307. I saw Art sitting in a wheelchair, and when I walked into his room, he greeted me with his usual jovial "Hello, Jimmy, my boy!"

"What's wrong, Art?" I asked, a little perplexed, as Art didn't look too sick to me.

"I got the big C," he replied. Then he went into a coughing fit. When he caught his breath, he turned to me and whispered in a raspy voice, "Jimmy, would you do me a favor?"

"Of course, Art. Anything for you."

I felt such empathy for him. Over the past year, Art had shared that he didn't have any close family members nearby. Most of his people had died or lived in Europe. I felt as though I had become a surrogate grandson and he was my surrogate grandfather.

"Jimmy, do you know Ben Silver, who works in the gift shop?"

"Yes, of course."

"Could you bring him up to see me when you can?"

I nodded. Art began to cough again. I rubbed his back and promised again that I would bring Ben to see him.

The next week, I checked to see if Ben was covering the gift shop. He was. I went in and said, "Art wants to see you for a minute. Do you mind coming to his room with me?"

Ben looked confused. "But I don't know Art. Why does he want to see me?"

I couldn't answer Ben's question. I shrugged my shoulders and said, "He really thinks it's important, I guess."

I hadn't seen Art for days, and when I entered his room, I was startled by his appearance. He looked thin and haggard—a mere shell of a man. I hardly recognized him. He certainly didn't look like the cheerful Art I knew so well. The room smelled like death, and the beeping of the monitors, along with the sound of the wheezing ventilator over Art's mouth, added to the disturbing scene. I could tell that Ben was very uncomfortable.

The two of us walked over to Art's bed. The patient seemed to be asleep, so I bent down and very softly called his name. Art opened his eyes, searching the room from side to side before focusing on my face. He didn't seem to recognize me.

"Hi Art. It's me, Jimmy. Remember me?"

Art looked at me as though he had never seen me before. Suddenly, a look of recognition came across his face. "Jimmy, Jimmy, did you do it? Did you bring him?"

"Yes, Art. He's right here."

Ben walked over to Art and practically yelled into his ear, "Hello, Art. It's me Ben. Nice to meet you. How're you doing?"

At that moment, Art grabbed Ben's hand and held it tight. He began crying. "Ben? Is that you?"

"Yes, Art. It's me. How can I help you?"

"Are you Jewish, Ben?"

This seemed like an odd question, considering almost every volunteer there had come from the local temple. I was curious to know why this meant so much to Art.

"Yes, Art," replied Ben. "Of course I am. Why do you ask?"

I pulled a chair next to the bed so Ben could sit and talk. As I watched the two elderly men, I strained to hear Art mumble his words to Ben.

"What, Art? I can't hear you. Speak up," said Ben.

"I need to let you know I'm sorry. I am so sorry. Will you please forgive me? I need to have your forgiveness. I cannot go until I have your forgiveness," Art pleaded.

"What are you talking about?"

"I need you to forgive me."

"Okay, I forgive you. I forgive you. But for what? What could you have done that you need me to forgive you for?"

Art took some deep breaths through the machine and then spoke softly. "I am sorry. During the war, I lived in Poland."

Ben's eyes lit up at this remark.

Art's head was bowed, and he stared at the sheet that covered his bed. "I was in the SS. I killed many Jews. I have never been able to forgive myself. I was wrong, and I am so sorry." Art's eyes filled with tears.

Ben and I were both shocked at Art's confession.

"I really need you to forgive me. Please."

Ben let go of Art's hand and sat back in his chair, a look of utter disbelief on his face.

Then Ben whispered, "My mother, my father, my uncle, my aunt, and my cousins were killed in the camps. For years I have spit on you people."

Ben bent his head down and started to cry. Several seconds went by. Then he raised his head and grabbed Art's hand.

"Yes, Art, my poor friend. I forgive you. I do forgive you, and the people who held your mind in prison. If I were not able to forgive you, I would be a criminal, just as you were when you killed my family. Yes, you are forgiven."

I could not believe that I was a witness to this incredible act between these two men. My eyes also filled with tears.

The two men sat for a while in silence. Then Ben got up, patted Art's hand, and left the room. I went over to Art and stroked his brow. I knew that he would be gone very soon.

"Good-bye, Art," I said.

He opened his eyes and looked into mine. "Good-bye, Jimmy. Thank you."

The act of forgiveness is one of the most difficult lessons to learn on the earth level, because it involves releasing ego and letting go of control. However, I cannot tell you how dramatic an effect it has in all areas of life, even if it happens at the end of life, as it did for Art. When we forgive, the door to happiness and health opens, bringing fulfillment, joy, and compassion. The act of forgiveness released both

Art's and Ben's souls from the atrocities that had scarred them for a lifetime.

UNTIL WE MEET AGAIN

So many upset people come to my workshops and demonstrations sharing their sad stories about not being physically present at the time of their loved one's passing. These people often spend a good portion of their time beating themselves up emotionally and mentally, unwilling or unable to forgive themselves for such an absence. I am asked over and over, "Does my wife (or husband, sister, mother, etc.) understand that I meant to be there? Does she (or he) forgive me for not being there?"

The following story shares some insights about just such a situation. It is my sincere hope that if you are in a similar mental and emotional state, the following message will bring peace to your heart and mind, so that you can forgive yourself for not being there.

I was the keynote speaker for "Celebrate Your Life," a conference I have participated in for the past thirteen years. At this particular event, the audience consisted of well over fifteen hundred people. In the middle of the message portion of the program, a spirit appeared to me wearing a green T-shirt and khaki pants. He told me that his wife was in the audience and that he needed to get a message to her right away. *Her life is falling apart, and I need to stop any further damage that she is creating with her thoughts.* He sent me a vision of a hospital, and I shared this vision with the audience.

"There is a man here whose wife is in trouble. He is showing me St. Joseph's Hospital. Does that make sense to someone, please?"

I gazed over the crowd. A woman with short brown hair, wearing dark-rimmed glasses and a pink print top, eventually stood up.

"I think that's me. I lost my husband. He was in St. Joseph's Hospital."

"He says that you have his golf clubs in the garage."

Assured that she was the right person, she quickly answered, "Yes! I was looking at them this morning and wondering if I should give them away or not."

Then the spirit filled me with a feeling of heaviness and lethargy, as if I were drugged. I became aware of little brown spots in his blood. I could sense how this man felt before he died.

"I feel that this man was heavily medicated before he left his body. Is that correct?"

"Yes, that's correct."

"His blood is filled with brown spots. Whenever I see this, it usually means cancer or a blood disease."

"Yes, he had prostate cancer." The woman told me her name was Shelly, and then she began to get extremely emotional.

"Your husband is telling me that your life is starting to spiral out of control. Is that right?"

"Yes. I guess you could say that. I miss him so much. Please tell him."

"You can tell him yourself, Shelly. He hears your thoughts all the time."

She nodded.

"You have been attracting some very negative people into your world. Your husband is telling me that someone in your life just stole something from you."

Shelly looked down. She understood what was being said to her.

"Your husband is telling me that you brought these people to you because you don't feel worthy of anything better. You are not caring for yourself. Is this true?"

"Yes, he's right. I became friendly with a gentleman because I felt sorry for him. He had no place to go, so I let him stay in a room in my house. One day I returned home, and he had left with many of my things."

Upon hearing this, the audience oohed their disapproval.

Shelly's husband was quick to add something else. I asked her, "Why are you blaming yourself for your husband's death?"

"Will he ever forgive me?"

"He is asking you, *For what?*"

"I wasn't there when he died. I hadn't made it back to the hospital, and I think he must have been angry with me for not being with him when he died. Does he know how sorry I am? I feel horrible. I have not been able to forgive myself for not being with him at the end."

Immediately, I felt extreme empathy for this poor woman. So many surviving loved ones feel terribly guilty for not being present when their loved ones pass over. From my years of communication, I know that our passing is divinely led. We will be present at a loved one's passing if we are meant to be there. We won't be at their death if it is deemed a better transition for the person's soul. We must remember that decisions about birth and death are made on a soul level. It is not unusual that we are completely unaware of these choices on the physical level. I often say to people that we come into this world alone and we must leave alone.

I looked back at Shelly and conveyed her husband's thoughts. "Your husband says to please realize that there is nothing to forgive. Please, please, do not beat yourself up for not being with him. Because he is in spirit, he feels everything with a stronger impact. He feels your self-loathing, and he feels terrible because he loves you so very much. He says that he wants to help you to realize that your unforgiving feelings are unnecessary. In fact, they make him feel worse!"

Then I turned to the audience to explain. "If you don't forgive yourself about this matter, you can bring yourself down to another level and draw lower elements to you. This is what Shelly has been doing."

I told Shelly, "Please honor your husband's request. Stop beating yourself up for not being there."

"Yes. I will," Shelly assured me.

Several years later, I was doing a book signing at a Barnes and Noble bookstore. Shelly came up to me and reminded me about the message I had given her from her husband. "I can't thank you enough for putting me back on the road to life. After the conference, I sat down and wrote my husband a letter and began the process of forgiving myself."

Shelly continued to tell me that after that she had felt such freedom. She was able to make clearer choices and drew more positive and loving events into her life.

"Since the reading, I took in a female roommate. She has become one of my best friends. We even opened a business together."

Shelly turned to a very tall man standing alongside her. "James, this is Todd."

Todd and I shook hands.

Shelly continued. "I met Todd through my new business. We have been going together for a couple of months and will probably be getting married next year."

I looked at her and said, "I am sure your husband couldn't be happier."

Shelly's life improved because she was able to forgive herself for something over which she had no control.

People often ask how to perform the act of forgiving, whether they have to actually speak to a person, and so forth. Forgiveness can be done in many ways. Like Shelly, you can write a card or letter and express your feelings to the other person, whether living or dead. You can send a picture and explain your feelings that way. You can buy a gift that the person would love. You can visualize a healing taking place between the two of you. Many times, I meditate and imagine a beautiful green healing crystal ball coming from my heart area and place the person or situation inside the crystal ball. I allow the healing energies to go directly to the person or situation.

Once we forgive, is it possible to forget? So many people say, "I can forgive, but not forget." When we forgive, we allow the other person to be human—in other words, have faults and make mistakes. We may not forget the situation, but we can forget the effects that the situation created in our relationship. Letting go of the need for revenge is the act of forgetting. It is an act of encouragement, support, and reinforcement. This allows the other person to rebuild, reconnect, and reestablish a loving, caring, and healthy relationship with you, others, and the world in which gifts, talents, and skills are freely appreciated and shared.

Self-forgiveness is one of the greatest gifts you can give yourself. You know you have been healed when you feel one with yourself. The part of you that held on to resentment and condemned you can now be made whole. When you forgive yourself, you return to your true self. You are in control of your reactions to life once again.

I went to bed thinking of this chapter on forgiveness. A friend with whom I had had difficulty popped into my mind. I asked for strength to forgive my friend and myself as I drifted off to sleep. When I awakened, something unexpected happened. I did not dream of the person I asked to forgive, but instead had the recurring dream about the mysterious man. It was the dream that I had been trying to analyze and understand for some time. Little did I know that I was about to embark on a whole new perception of the spirit world and myself.

SIX

Karma

*The most important thing in life is to learn how to
give out love, and to let it come in.*

—Morrie Schwartz

As you know, there is no sense of time in dreams. They appear to us as moments. In my dream I was still in the hospital room. The same figure of the man I had seen the last time in my dream came toward me. I was now able to make out his face. I had seen him before, but couldn't remember where. He was smiling at me, and I could see that there were others standing behind him. Each one transmitted a feeling of joy and happiness as though it was some sort of reunion. I couldn't wait to be with them and join their party. I knew and felt I was being given a message, but was unsure what it was. Deep down I knew I had been with these people before and that we shared some kind of karma with each other.

And then it happened! I was suddenly standing across the room looking at a hospital bed. There was a woman in the bed. She was talking to the man and the group of people. Then in an instant she floated out of her body to join the group. I was witnessing a death right before my eyes. In my dream I wondered to myself why this was happening. I would like to say it was symbolic, but it felt as if I was being shown this scene for a reason, as if someone was trying to tell me something. I still didn't know what. I could not make out the woman's face, yet somehow I felt I knew her. I also felt we had a positive karmic connection with one another. But who was she? Then, as quickly as it started, the dream was over. I was still left with questions.

In the past thirty years, the concept of karma has made its way into mainstream American culture. However, most people do not really understand it, because they usually think of karma as a kind of punishment. Karma is not punishment; it is a concept, originating from an ancient Hindu belief, about the consequences of actions. The idea of karma is part of various religious ideologies, such as Hinduism, Jainism, Sikhism, Buddhism, Spiritualism, and numerous New Age philosophies. It is also found in the Bible: "A man reaps what he sows" (Gal. 6:7, NIV). Although the explanation of karma is slightly different in the various religious traditions, the idea behind it is basically the same. It is defined as the cause and effect of an action, or the principle that what one actively chooses to do will define the experiences the soul must go through in the present life or future lives.

Karma has always been intertwined with another ancient concept—that of reincarnation. Other than Christians, most people around the globe believe in reincarnation. The idea of rebirth was removed from Christian doctrine in 325 CE at the Council of Nicea. We could speculate about why it was removed, but I believe that reincarnation didn't sit well with church fathers. They wanted to control their congregants in the here and now and not let them believe their sins could be corrected in another life.

Over the centuries, religious aspects of karma have been misinterpreted as laws of morality. In truth, karma has nothing to do with morality; it is a natural universal law of cause and effect. Simply put, what you give out you will get back. When you do something, a result must follow. If something happens, something or someone caused it to happen. For instance, you go through a red light and get hit by the car that has the right-of-way—that's karma. When we understand the full scope of the concept of karma, we realize that each of us is solely responsible for our life, including everything that we create in thought, word, and deed.

My personal view of karma is a compilation of various disciplines blended with what I have learned from the spirit world on the subject. There seems to be no judgment at all attached to karma in the spirit world. Karma is neutral; it is merely a tool for learning and having experiences. All choices are derived from either love or fear. Love is a pure high energy; fear is a lower fragmented energy. We often refer to these qualities as either positive or negative.

When a soul journeys on earth, it needs to learn many lessons of all different types. It needs to wholly understand an experience from all sides. Some might have to learn about selflessness, so their Higher Selves, or soul consciousness, may place them in situations where they must give and do more than what they are comfortable with. Others may be placed in positions of incredible wealth. The lesson for each one is to see what a person does in a specific situation. Do the wealthy ones share their money with those in need, or do they hold on to it for fear it will run out? Do the uncomfortable ones break out of their comfort zones and succeed despite roadblocks and limitations?

Many also confuse karma with fate or destiny. Be aware that the two are very different. Fate or destiny can be changed, but karma cannot. For instance, a person is destined to be a successful and well-known singer, but he has to work through his past karma of releasing addictions. If he chooses to become an alcoholic once again in his present life, he has not learned his karmic lesson, and by that choice his destiny has been changed. On the other hand, had he overcome his addiction, had he learned his karmic lesson, he could have realized his destiny. There is certainly no way to *prove* that karma exists, but things do happen as a result of the choices we make. By constantly creating karma, we have within us the ability to change the outcome of our future. As I have said many times, we are responsible for our actions and the results they bring. Put it another way, if you break it, you pay for it!

Coincidence or Karma?

Most of us look at events like winning the lottery, thinking of a friend and then meeting her that very same day, or finding the perfect gift that just happens to be at a store you accidentally walked into as coincidences. But I believe there are no such things as coincidences. As much as we would like to believe it, nothing really happens by chance. Karma, not chance, is the reason.

I recently went on a trip to New York, and during my stay a series of quite unexplainable situations occurred. I remember the day I looked out the window of my Midtown Manhattan hotel and watched a torrent of rain flooding the city. It was eleven o'clock in the morning, and I had an early lunch date with a friend twenty blocks away.

I walked out of the hotel and asked the doorman, "Do you think I can get a cab? I'm late for an appointment."

He said, "No, Mr. Van Praagh, it's impossible to catch a cab in this rain. Perhaps you can try going down to Sixth Avenue and get one there."

"Thanks." I began a fast pace down the street in the pouring rain.

As I walked, I sent a mental message to my friend's husband, who had passed, and asked if he could please get me a cab, unsure if that was even possible from his lofty perch. When I got to the corner, I raised my hand up high into the onslaught of falling water, and a cab stopped short in front of me. I was surprised and grateful at the same time. I quickly opened the door and climbed inside, praising the driver and thanking him for stopping for me. I have always made it a habit to bring a little ray of sunshine and support to everyone I meet along my journey.

"Where are you from?" I asked the cabbie.

"Jaipur," he replied in a lilting Indian accent.

I then shared my many activities during my visit to the Big Apple. He also shared how his morning went, which mostly consisted of waiting in line at JFK Airport. "Too many grumpy people," the cabbie informed me.

I kidded him about New Yorkers, and he laughed at my joy.

As he pulled up to my destination, I said, "Thank you. I appreciate your getting me here safe and sound. How much is that?"

He turned to me and smiled. "No charge. You have made my day by making me feel better, so I am not charging you."

Having grown up in New York and having gone back and forth from coast to coast over the past thirty years, I have heard many words come out of a cabbie's mouth, but never those.

I responded, "No, that is very kind of you. I appreciate the thought, but this is your job, and I want to honor that."

And with that, I reached into my pocket for my wallet and found that I had left the hotel without any money at all! My face turned red at the thought of telling the cabbie I had no money. Then suddenly I looked down, and on the seat was a bank card with several twenties wrapped around it. I looked up to heaven and said, "Thank you. I will put it back." I took a twenty and paid the cabbie. When I got back to the hotel, I called the bank to report the lost card. Now, was that a coincidence?

The next day in the city, my laptop went dead, and I had to buy a new battery. I asked the hotel concierge, "Is there a computer store in the area?"

He said, "There's one on Madison and Sixty-First."

I walked toward Madison, but midway there my mind went completely blank, and I forgot which direction I was headed. I asked my guides to give me a sign, so I knew I was going in the right direction. I looked up and saw that I was standing in front of the HarperCollins building. HarperCollins is the wonderful American publisher of the book you are currently reading. I knew I was headed in the right direction. Was that a coincidence or a sign from the spiritual world?

When I got back to Los Angeles, I had to meet with a producer named Tom Burnell in Santa Monica. The address was 1520 Olympic Boulevard. Since I was not familiar with the area, I programmed the information into the navigation system of my car. My friend Brian sat in the passenger seat and kept me company on the ninety-minute trek north from my home in Orange County. When we approached our Santa Monica destination, the GPS operator reported, "Your destination is on the right." However, when we looked around, we were not at the Olympic Boulevard meeting place. Instead, we were in front of a television studio. It was not just any television studio, but the one that tapes the *Chelsea Lately* show on E! TV.

"This blows my mind!" I shrieked. "I'm supposed to be here tomorrow for the show!" (I was scheduled as a guest.) The restaurant where I was to meet Tom was twenty blocks away.

Was this a coincidence? How can I explain that the navigation system brought me to the place I was supposed to be at the next day?

One of the very first psychics I ever met, Dolores North, told me something I remember to this day and quote to all my students. She said, "If you are on the path you are meant to be on, everything falls into place; the Universe is telling you that. If you are not on your right path, you will experience roadblocks all along the way, and this is also the Universe telling you to stop, look, and ask if this is where you are supposed to be." After experiencing the truth of this comment time and again, I agree that we do have a particular destiny, and we can either travel the path to it or veer off and do something completely different. It is our free will. However, this idea does not preclude our going through lessons, whether difficult or easy. After all, we have come to earth to expand our soul's understanding and grow to be great spirits, so lessons are a must.

Finally, can the spirit world get involved in our daily lives and help us move toward our destiny? Can spirits assist us by helping to make things happen? Can they prevent horrendous experiences as well? I have asked these questions of spirits, and the responses are pretty much unanimous. They agree that they can never interfere in a person's karma, because it is the natural development of events necessary for a soul's learning. However, they can indeed *influence* a soul to use love in all of its choices. But we still make the decisions.

Often people ask me why everything is so difficult in their lives. I tell them that learning is never easy. The situations and people in our life that cause us the most trouble are also our greatest teachers. In order to deal with adversity or overcome a situation, we are forced to go deep within our soul and pull out a strength we may never have experienced before. Because the purpose of our time here is optimum growth and understanding, spirits want us to succeed, but they cannot give us the answers to our tests. Spirits are very aware of our earthly situations and can guide us in the right direction, but we have to be open to all of our choices and make them through love. This was certainly made evident in the following reading.

A BROTHER'S GUIDANCE

I was doing one of my very popular spiritual cruises. At one of my daily demonstrations, I had just finished a group meditation, when I looked to the right side of the audience and observed a redheaded man sitting very patiently. Behind him I noticed blinking white lights. Mediums usually refer to these as spirit lights and have actually captured them on film. When I see them, I know that a spirit is beginning to materialize behind an individual.

"Sir, may I come to you?" I asked as I walked to the red-headed gentleman.

"Yes."

"What is your name, please?"

"Gregory Hobbs."

I ask a person's name for two reasons. First, I must hear an individual's voice in order to tune into his or her energy field. Second, it focuses the person's attention on what I have to say.

As Gregory said his name, a tall, ruddy-complexioned man came into focus behind him. He looked just like Gregory.

"Do you have an older brother who passed?"

"Yes, I do. His name was Russell."

I suddenly felt a pain in my chest, which told me how Russell died. "Did your brother have a heart attack?"

"Yes, he did," Gregory answered with surprise in his voice.

"He is telling me that you still communicate with him—cursing him out. Is this true?"

Gregory seemed uncomfortable and a bit embarrassed. "Yeah, I guess you could say that."

Russell filled my head with a myriad of thoughts. "Your brother is telling me that he was your older brother and always took care of you. In a way, he was like a father to you, because he was always looking out for you. Is that right?"

"Yeah, I guess so. He was my older brother and always kept me out of trouble. I was cursing him out, because I recently got into an accident and almost got killed. I said, like hey bro, couldn't you have warned me about it? I thought you were my guardian angel."

Russell answered his brother, *I did warn you, but you wouldn't listen.* I asked Gregory, "Several months ago, did you see a red light on your dash telling you to check your brakes?"

Gregory had to think a little. "Yeah, actually I did."

His brother continued showing me visions. "Did you also go for a checkup for your engine, and you were told by the mechanic something about your brakes?"

"Yes," Gregory replied sheepishly.

I continued, "Also, now this is weird, but I am being shown a billboard and it says, 'Fix your brakes.'"

Gregory shook his head and mumbled, "Yeah, that's right. I was at a red light and looked over to the right and there was an advertisement about brakes."

"Your brother made you look at that sign."

The look on Gregory's face made me think he knew what I was about to say next.

"Your car went over a hill because you were going too fast and the brakes failed. Is that right?"

"You got it."

"Your brother is telling me that your lesson is responsibility. He couldn't make you fix the brakes, and unfortunately you had to live with the result of your action or lack of action. The choice was yours. That was your karma. He tried to help, but he could not get in the way of your learning."

When I looked at Gregory, a lightbulb seemed to go off in his head. I guessed that he had finally gotten it!

Gregory looked up to the ceiling and said, "Thanks for keeping an eye out for me, bro. I love you, man!"

Group Karma

Besides individual karma, there is also group karma. Groups include ethnicities, families, nations, businesses or industries, and various kinds of social networks. All of us choose to come back to certain families, because our souls have a karmic connection with each other. We all know that wonderful expression: "You can pick your friends, but you can't pick your family." Well, in truth, we do pick our families! We decide in between lives that there are certain important group karmic experiences we have to learn and undertake in order to evolve spiritually.

So, we decide which roles we will assume that will give the group the optimum number of possibilities to manifest those various lessons. Simply put, those souls we call our family (including our extended family and close friends) have spent many lifetimes with us on this earth learning various lessons.

In one lifetime you might have been the father, in another the child, and in still another the grandparent. The role doesn't matter. There is a group learning dynamic, and the objective is for you to take on these various roles, so that you can learn and evolve as a more rounded and experienced being. Experience is the greatest teacher.

I have observed many family relationships in which for no reason the mother and daughter, or two brothers, or the father and son have never been able to get along. Most do not understand why this is so, but they feel it down to the core of their being. In this life, their souls have returned to work out their relationship and to understand one another.

Whenever I explain to students what I mean by group or collective karma, I like to use the following illustrations. The first one is feeling the collective energy of a group of people. Whenever I appear on stage before a group, I can tell within ten seconds what kind of an audience it is. I know if the people are receptive, closed-minded, fun-loving, serious, grief-stricken, nonbelieving, or just plain curious. How can I tell? By feeling the energy the group is sending out. Each of us is an individual with our own identifiable energy. However, when we come together as an audience, no matter what the situation is, we become part of a group dynamic. Think of times that you were at a party. Good party or dull party? The group dynamic creates the atmosphere. You can sense if the room is filled with happy people or unhappy, depressed people by the energy generated in the room.

The second is an analogy. Think of group karma as a big vat of soup. Individuals are the vegetables in the soup. Each vegetable is an important ingredient and will either make the soup taste good or bad.

The soup would not be very good if the flavors of the ingredients clashed with rather than enhanced one another.

People are also here to learn and work out karmic obligations by being part of a specific racial, ethnic, religious, or minority group. By placing yourself in particular company, you will be afforded situations only available by being in that unique situation. Besides individual karma, there are group interactions and dynamics constantly at play in a soul's growth and understanding.

I also believe we come into a particular country because we have a karmic connection with that country in one way or another. At the same time, a country must fulfill its own karmic obligations and evolve. We, as individuals of that country, are part of its evolution. We must remember that nations as well as individuals do good or bad things. Each action by a country creates a rippling effect, and each country has a chance to do the right thing.

The key in understanding a nation's karma is knowing the motive behind its leaders' actions. There have been many stories and articles over the years speculating on George W. Bush's presidency and the karma he has created for the United States. What was Bush's motive for going to war in Iraq? Was it the best of all the alternatives available? Was his motive pure? Was it for the good of humankind, or was it negative karma stemming from greed and past life conflicts? Was it really for the independence of the Iraqi people, or was it for the control of oil?

From an astrological point of view, Mr. Bush has a very afflicted chart. Born under the sign of Cancer, he is very sensitive and concerned about family values. But it also reveals that he is impulsive and sees the world from a narrow perspective. Karmicly, battles are a part of his past. An astrology chart, like many other metaphysical vehicles, is a tool to gain insight into a person's personality and demeanor. One area of a chart reveals the soul's karmic propensities. His chart shows that he came back here to attain a powerful position in the world and was given many opportunities to rise up and utilize the higher aspects of his being, such as understanding, empathy, and sensitivity. Clearly, he had been given the choice to change his karma from the past and transform. Unfortunately, his decision was made, and it has cost many lives.

AMERICA'S SWEETHEART

Years ago, I did a reading for a famous television star. For the book, I will call her Melanie. This celebrity's television show was quite popular for many, many years and is still in syndication around the world. Melanie had two children, and the moment her older daughter was born, she knew instinctively that this was going to be one of the hardest karmic lessons of her lifetime. From the moment her daughter could talk, she was demanding and unruly and acted out, all to get attention.

Before the reading began, Melanie confided to me, "James, the day she was born, I looked at her and said to myself, I know this one. And oh, she's going to cause me heartache. I need to know what's going on between the two of us."

Immediately, I saw a female spirit with long, wiry salt-and-pepper hair standing behind Melanie. The spirit had very powerful thoughts, and she told me, *I did what you are doing now.*

"There's a woman here who is wearing a flowing multicolored caftan robe. She seems quite larger than life. She is telling me that she did what I am doing. Her name is Dinah or Dana."

"Oh my God. That's Dede, my psychic."

"Well, she does get her thoughts across very clearly."

"Yes, that's Dede. She always said what was on her mind."

"She wants you to know," I continued, "that she is your guide now. She keeps an eye on you and makes sure that you are not getting in over your head."

"Thank you, Dede. I can use your help."

I listened to Dede's thoughts, which were coming to me fast and furiously. "She is telling me about your daughter now. She says that you are afraid of your daughter. Is this true?"

Melanie lowered her gaze. "Yes, James, she terrorizes me." After a beat, she added, "What could I have possibly done to her to deserve such treatment?"

I was a little taken aback by this comment.

"Dede tells me that you had many lifetimes with your daughter, and many of these lives were powerful ones. You both were important people."

"That makes sense, don't you think, James?"

"Dede says that because you were powerful in those other lives, your daughter is actually jealous of you in this life because she is not the star."

"Oh my God!" Melanie shrieked. "No wonder she treats me so badly."

"Dede wants you to be careful. Your daughter still has a grudge against you from a previous life. You and she have been pitted against one another many times. In the last life together, you were a king and she was your daughter. She tried to get you killed, so that she could take your power. You found out and banished her to an island for the rest of her life."

I was surprised to hear this. I could tell that the communication unnerved Melanie.

"Dede is saying that your daughter never made it to the island. On her way, a group of villagers killed her because they loved the king so much and hated the daughter for trying to get rid of him. When you learned that your daughter was murdered, you blamed yourself. You died of a broken heart the following morning."

Both Melanie and I were speechless at this point.

"Dede says that the two of your have a lot of karmic lessons to learn. Your daughter has to learn to deal with your popularity and not be jealous of your fame. You two have set up a scenario in this life, so that you both can learn how to love one another no matter what positions you have in life. One more thing. She says she is always with you and is watching your back."

Then the psychic spirit faded away.

So you can see how karmic patterns are played out. If more of us are mindful that we have been with our family members over and over again, the lessons won't be so difficult to comprehend, and certain behavior can be encouraged while other behavior can be curbed.

THERE ARE NO ACCIDENTS

According to Buddhism, karma is the sum total of all of our previous actions and our current impulses. I look at it from this perspective. If we are all God, or a spark of God, and God is Love, and we live our lives in a godlike way, which means demonstrating Love in everything we do, then we create positive karma. The results of our actions will be loving. All things done with love help us to see our lessons more clearly and fully appreciate them for what they are worth.

When a soul wants to learn more, gain experience, and evolve as a spiritual being, it is reincarnated into a new body. Reincarnation seems a reasonable way for a soul to have an opportunity to develop further. The soul can work out any missed opportunities and bring balance to the karma of a previous life's cycle. The time in between incarnations is not set per se, but a soul does use "time" in the spirit world as preparation for a new life.

A soul seems to make a decision to reincarnate at the time of conception by the parents. At that moment, the parents open the channel of expression. A soul pattern seems to form by mingling with the soul patterns of the parents. I do believe that this is part of our soul group connection with our parents in which we take on some of their karma in our incarnations. This idea is also mentioned in the Bible: "He

[God] punishes the children and their children for the sins of the fathers" (Exod. 34:7, NIV). I wonder if that is why toward the latter part of our lives, we often find that we behave just like our parents. The wonderful sleeping prophet Edgar Cayce said during one of his trances, "Family is just the river through which the soul flows."

Through the years, thousands of people have experienced past-life recall, whether by having déjà vu or a vivid dream, being drawn to a particular place for no apparent reason, or being hypnotically regressed. Our past-life experiences are indelibly imprinted in our soul fabric. When accessed, the soul memory can reveal pivotal prior lifetimes and expose the karma we are currently working through from a past life.

Many people with whom I have worked have asked their loved ones in the spirit world why certain events were happening in their current lives or why certain people were behaving badly toward them. Often spirits answer that a balancing of a previous incarnation is needed. To put it another way, a debt must be paid back in order for a soul to be made whole. The following is a remarkable example of how souls come together to work out their karmic debts from the past. It is another one of my readings that has stayed with me.

Years ago, a group of mothers came to see me at one of my meetings in a hotel in Laguna Beach. After our initial introductions and a brief meditation, I saw a young man with wavy brown hair standing behind one of the mothers.

"Bonnie, I have a young man here. He is your son, I believe. He is around nineteen and wears a T-shirt with a gun pictured on it."

Bonnie's eyes welled up with tears, and she grabbed hold of the hand of the woman next to her. "Yes, that's my son Toby."

I started to feel the impact of Toby's death. Suddenly, my head felt like it was spinning, and then everything went black. "Did he die in a car accident?"

Bonnie and the woman beside her nodded their heads in unison.

"He mentions that he is here with the other ladies's sons. They all knew each other from school and hung out together. They were fascinated with guns, the movie *Platoon*, and Vietnam. Is this correct?"

At this point the other two mothers, Patty and Sharon, sitting on either side of Bonnie, raised their hands as a sign to me that they were present.

Patty shared, "My son was also fascinated with Vietnam and *Platoon*."

Sharon added, "They were like the Three Musketeers. They went everywhere together and were fascinated with war stories, especially about Vietnam."

As she was speaking, the other two young male spirits showed up. All three were the same age. They seemed to be happy together, as if they were always meant to be together.

I asked the three young men to show me their accident. The picture was quickly implanted in my mind. I could see the three boys in the front seat of a black Jeep Cherokee. They were driving too fast, especially around the curves. Toby was laughing as he bent his head to turn the radio up louder. Just then, another car coming from the opposite direction caused Toby to grab the steering wheel, and the Jeep veered out of the way and into a telephone pole. The car burst into flames. All three young men were trapped inside and died in the burning vehicle.

As I explained what I saw to the rest of the people in the room, the mothers clutched one another's hands for support. Some people were crying.

Bonnie then asked me, "Why did they have to die like that—in a car crash?"

"Your son is telling me that it had to be that way. It was a karmic debt that needed to be repaid."

Then I said to all three of the mothers, "The girls in the other car were not hurt. Is that right?"

They nodded.

I asked the boys for clarification about the karma that had to be repaid.

"Your sons are telling me that they served together in the Vietnam war before this incarnation. This was probably in the late 1960s. Now I am getting a picture of a full moon. I see. This took place during the Chinese New Year. The three soldiers were riding around in their jeep looking for gooks, they are saying. They were all drunk from celebrating. They found a man and woman, a husband and wife, hiding in a car. The three soldiers jumped out of their jeep and taunted the couple, calling them names. Then they began shooting at the car, and the vehicle went up in flames. The two people were trapped inside. Oh my God! The three of them just stood by and watched the couple die in the fire."

I had to take a few minutes to digest everything that was being shown to me. The rest of the crowd sat silently. It was an unbelievably horrible picture. The three mothers were all crying as they heard how cruel their sons had been in another life.

I turned to the mothers and said, "There really are no accidents. The car accident in this life was not the fault of the two girls in the other car. Thankfully, those girls did not even sustain a scratch."

"But if they died in Vietnam, why did they have to die again in this life?" asked Sharon. "Wasn't their karma repaid in that war?"

"Not necessarily," I replied.

Then I asked the young spirits if they were drafted. "Toby is telling me that they all enlisted in the war. They were very gung ho about going into the military, using weapons, and fighting for their country. Their karma was not connected with enlisting in the war. Their motivation for that was honest. However, their motivation for killing innocent people was not. It was unwarranted and heartless. That was their karmic debt."

Then the young men told their mothers how sorry they were for causing them pain. "Toby is saying, *Please don't cry for us. We had to pay it back. Now we are free.*"

Several months after the messages from her son, Bonnie visited the home of the two girls, whom she had also known, as they were school-mates of her son and the other two boys. She felt she needed to do this as a final act of healing. Missy Holmes, the mother of the girls, answered the door, and Bonnie thanked her for letting her visit. The two women spoke about the accident. As Bonnie told Missy about my reading and how the boys were involved in Vietnam, Missy contrib-uted some valuable information of her own.

"It's funny you should talk about your son's fascination with Viet-nam. My two girls are also fascinated with Vietnam. They want to visit it one day. And they are scared to death of fire to the point of obsession."

"Really?"

"They have even put fire ropes out their windows in case of a fire. They are so afraid of being trapped."

Bonnie, not knowing how to explain the synergy of Toby's life with the lives of these two girls, hoped that her son would be able to help the girls overcome their fear of fire from his place in the spirit world.

Perhaps the two girls in the accident were the husband and wife burned to death in Vietnam that day. We will never really know. How-ever, what does matter is that those three young men were responsible for their hateful actions. They had to reap what they had sown.

Bear in mind that karma is not a punishment, but a way of manag-ing our actions and reactions. Karma is also an educational tool to help us evolve spiritually and to balance out the results of all the ac-tions we have generated that are out of harmony with the law of love. We are given many opportunities in this life to clean up negative karma from previous existences and, yes, the spirit world has made it very clear to me that as souls we have lived many times and in many different places.

I remember a time when I was stopped at a red light. The car in front of me had a bumper sticker I will never forget. It read, "How you treat me is your karma. How I react is mine." I love that saying, and keep the idea in mind every day.

Knowing that we have karma is one thing, but how do we deal with it? That is the focus of the next chapter.

PART THREE

i can see
CLEARLY

SEVEN

Overcoming Obstacles

Success is not measured by the heights one attains,
but by the obstacles one overcomes in its attainment.

—Booker T. Washington

How many times have you looked at a situation in your life and wondered, "How could God do this to me? There is no possible way I can get out of this!" Perhaps, you just broke down in tears, thinking you were stuck in that situation and had no idea of what would happen to you and your family.

Whenever I think the world is a difficult place and everything seems overwhelming, I cannot help but humble myself and remember one single woman whose courage triumphed against all odds. She was one of the greatest spiritual teachers who ever lived and is a perfect example of how to overcome any obstacle in your path. At the age of one and a half, she became blind and deaf. She used her obstacle not as a crutch, but as a vehicle to open the door to understanding herself and to share her insights and knowledge with her fellow beings. She was able to encourage others to live the fullness of life. If we could see even a glimmer of what she was able to do despite her affliction, we would appreciate every moment of our lives. Her name is Helen Keller. She said: "When one door of happiness closes, another opens; but often we look so long at the closed door that we do not see the one that has been opened for us."

By now in your journey through the words on these pages, I hope you have reached a moment of reevaluation. By reviewing the points about life and death and the choices that create the in-between life, you may well have a very different perspective on, or at least some insight into, how to choose to behave in life's situations. I know that with this new understanding you can begin to live a more productive life, in a more responsible manner, and release old patterns of control and negative behaviors.

In life there are always obstacles. As one of my guides, RaMa, once told me, obstacles are opportunities to learn more about ourselves and the world in which we live. Life would certainly be boring, and we would not grow, if there were no disagreements, conflicts, and unexpected traumas in our lives. Learning to overcome them is what life is all about. When things seem bad, I always remember a song that pulled Annie out of the doldrums: "The Sun Will Come Out Tomorrow." It's true.

Stop for a moment and seriously think about your predicament. There may be days when you can barely lift your head off the pillow in the morning, because all appears to be lost. But you know, as part of your human makeup, you have a survival instinct deep down in your core. You want to keep hope alive for a new day, and on that new day you may see something different about your circumstance that you didn't see the day before. Or someone calls and presents you with a new opportunity.

Nothing is so bad that we cannot grow from it, but we need a good attitude. When dealing with obstacles, we must generate a sense of self-awareness and self-belief and choose the way to react from our truth. We can uniquely respond to a situation with our own mindful thoughts. When we know that we have such power to change our perspective, we feel in control of a situation, not that the situation is in control of us.

Never give in to failure. That is not what you want. You must realize that it is not the end of the world, that there are always other prospects coming your way. You can have things exactly the way you have dreamed of them, no matter what that dream may be.

By defining some of the basic obstacles and their origins, I hope to give you a way to remove your blockages and acquire a fresh outlook. It helps to keep an open mind and heart and have patience, strength, and individuality in all that you do. When you perceive yourself more clearly, you will be able to recognize all those who love you as well.

Fear

I covered many points about fear in Chapter 3. Fear is a normal emotional response that is part of our survival instinct. But fear directed toward anything other than survival is pure illusion that we have stored in our minds. Fear can signal escape or avoidance of an issue. It also makes for unnecessary worry. When we fear something, we tend to make it seem worse than it actually is. In other words, we blow a situation or circumstance out of proportion and make a mountain out of a molehill.

Most of our fears have been instilled in us from the belief systems of our parents or our religion or from other people's skewed perceptions. Fear can motivate us to get ahead in life, because we are afraid of failure. Or it can hold us back from realizing our dreams, desires, and goals because "we don't think we can do it." For many, it seems easier to be afraid than to believe in success. We need to honestly face our fears by writing them down and looking at them *realistically*—and that means not rationalizing them, minimizing them, or succumbing to their power in our lives.

Attitude

Attitude is vastly important, because it presents your image to the world and is the driving force behind behavior. Your attitude influences your world and everything you do in it. It defines the energy you send out and, in turn, takes shape and color in your circumstances. If you have a positive attitude, you are more welcoming and people are drawn to you. A positive attitude opens you to the flow of life. If you are depressed, angry, and unhappy, no one wants to be around you. You literally push people and opportunities away.

The wonderful thing is that you have the freedom to choose which attitude you want to adopt. There is no perfect way; each way is unique to each individual. For instance, let's say your supervisor at work cuts your hours. You can choose the attitude that he or she has been unfair and, therefore, you are not going to work as hard. Your attitude demonstrates that you are not as involved in your job as you think or say you are. On the other hand, you can adopt an attitude of understanding; perhaps you don't know everything that is happening in the company, and cutting hours is necessary to keep everyone working. Another thing to keep in mind: you don't have to take everything in life so personally. Some things are part of a bigger picture. When you can think, "I know it will work perfectly, as it is meant to," it usually does—karmicly speaking, that is.

Knowing that you can choose how to react is especially important when unexpected problems occur. Remind yourself of techniques to keep a positive attitude. In doing so, you are guaranteed to have a happier life.

MY FATHER'S APPROVAL

One remarkable story regarding the affirming attributes of attitude comes from a message I gave to twenty-two-year-old Dean. I had a chance meeting with him prior to my television show *Beyond* in 2002. In the development stage of my show, several of the producers wanted to familiarize themselves with my work, so they arranged a demonstration with a group of five people unknown to me. I remember walking onto the sound stage and seeing three women and two men sitting in a row of chairs. They all appeared to be in their early twenties.

"Hello. I'm James," I said to them.

They all responded, but one young man in particular stood out. He said, "Hi James. It's a pleasure to meet you. You do such wonderful work. Thank you for all you do."

What struck me about this young man was his smile and warm, friendly attitude. Dean just exuded charm and magnetism. He reminded me of a younger version of Hugh Grant.

As I began the reading for the five audience members, Dean's father appeared. He stood on the right side of the young man and seemed to be standoffish and dubious about what was taking place.

"Dean, your father is here. He seems to be a little skeptical about being here."

"Sounds like him. He never quite believed in many things."

"Your father is saying you have a gift, and he didn't know it until after he passed."

"A gift? What gift?"

"He says that you have a positive outlook on life. He says that you always had this gift, even when you were a child. People always said you were a nice kid, and your father thought you were a jerk for being so nice."

I could see that Dean was a little confused by his father's remarks.

I continued, "He didn't know how to deal with you when he was alive. He's sorry that he made fun of you a lot."

"That's okay, Dad. I know I was different."

"Your father says that he was worried that people would take advantage of your good nature. In his own way he was trying to protect you."

"I was always a happy-go-lucky kind of kid. I guess I was born that way."

I nodded. "Thank you," I said. "Your dad says that your optimism is going to go far in this world, and that many doors will open for you. You will have a wonderful career, and he's going to enjoy seeing you get ahead in life."

Dean beamed. "Hey, that's great news."

"Yes," I said. "Your dad says that he is watching you and is learning so much from you. He says he wished he learned from you while he was alive."

"He is?!" Dean exclaimed. "That's so funny."

"Why do you say that?" I asked.

"My father used to say that I saw the world through rose-colored glasses. He thought I would never get ahead with such a dumb attitude. And now he's learning from me? That's so ironic."

I smiled at Dean. "We are always learning, whether here or there. Spirits learn from us just as we learn from them."

Dean looked up. "I love you, Dad."

Then I felt the presence of other spirits, and I went on to speak to the rest of the makeshift audience.

The other day as I was channel surfing on the TV, I stopped to watch a new show. I couldn't believe what I saw. To my surprise, the lead actor was Dean, the young man with the great attitude. All I could think was, "Good for you, Dean. Those rose-colored glasses paid off."

Emotions

We are naturally emotional beings. Our emotions can be a guide to doing the right thing, or they can be a hindrance by getting in the way of our decisions. Depending on the amount and type, emotions can and do often hold us back from living up to our potential. When we get overwhelmed with negative emotions like depression, fear, anger, worry, and so forth, we immediately feel under attack and trapped. These emotions force us to focus on what is presumably wrong, and we immediately feel something needs to be fixed. Negative emotions drain us; they bring us down psychologically as well as physically. Our brain hormones change. We are easily lulled into victim consciousness, because our point of view becomes limited. Our bodies tighten and our heads hang down. We want to lie down and pull the covers over us. We are in a slump.

Positive emotions like love, forgiveness, and joy provide our lives with growth and expansion. These emotions help us to see and discover far-reaching possibilities. We all know what it feels like when we are overjoyed at something. We feel as if we had the strength of a lion and that anything is possible. We smile; we dance; we enthusiastically shout out; we are in such a happy space. The more positive our emotions, the healthier we are in body, mind, and spirit. We are more tolerant, more creative, and more able to fully involve ourselves in the incredible opportunities life presents to us.

I tell people that whenever they feel sad and depressed to close their eyes and think of one thing that makes them happy. This could be a childhood memory, a joke, or a funny movie—something that makes them laugh and feel good. Laughter is the best medicine, because it immediately changes our energy. It has not only a psychological effect, but a physical one too. It actually changes our brain chemistry, and it does so without any artificial stimulants or drugs. I often find that, whenever I am in a place where the energy is way too heavy and fearful, whether it is an elevator, taxi, or workshop, I break out in song. I sing to my heart's delight. Usually, this brings a smile (probably some shock as well) to everyone's face. People laugh, and the energy is changed.

Stress

Simply put, stress is the opposite of relaxation, yet it's a normal part of life. Stress is a physical response to how we perceive a situation. Some stress is beneficial. For instance, you have an important project at work; you can utilize creative stress to push on and deliver a great product or performance by the appointed deadline. And the fight-or-flight aspect of the survival instinct, although stress-inducing, protects us from danger and assists us to live safely in an unfriendly environment. A little stress is okay, but a lot of stress is deadly.

Unhealthy stress occurs when we feel out of control and powerless over things that are affecting our lives. For instance, a woman juggles being a mother, a lawyer, a friend, an involved citizen, and a workout junkie. She attempts to give each activity her complete best. A man who is the head of his own company constantly plays a balancing act between the pressures of being an entrepreneur, a husband, and a father. Both people are under too much stress.

Stress needs to be modulated; it cannot run your life. If you have too much stress in your life, the end result can be physical ailments such as headaches, insomnia, digestive problems, mood swings, chest pains, and more. When I scan people's auras and see an overwhelming amount of energy around the head area, I know that this means too much stress, too much worry, too much to take care of, and too much to be responsible for.

How can you deal with stress? Here are a few suggestions:

Reflect on your activities and goals. Are they realistic, or are you setting yourself up for disappointment?

Simplify your life by delegating responsibilities. You don't need to do everything!

Exercise regularly to relieve stress and heal the body.

Take up an enjoyable hobby like gardening or painting.

Write down a list of priorities. Get the stuff out of your head and onto paper, so you'll have a clear picture of what's important.

Stop trying to be everything to everyone. Just be you!

By managing stress, you'll get a lot more done in a more efficient way, and life will be far more enjoyable.

Money

Money is a wonderful tool and a great energy source. However, for many people money is an incredible obstacle, because it is so confining. Money can obstruct the ability to clearly see the bigger picture and understand the greater meaning of life.

We have all known or heard about people who have great fortunes at their disposal. Yet these millionaires are some of the most unhappy and unfulfilled people on earth. Just having money doesn't necessarily mean you have wealth. Money is a material object. Being wealthy is an attitude.

The majority of us live month to month, paying bills and, if we are fortunate, putting away some money for the future. However, most of the time, enough isn't enough. We always want more, as if money is the great panacea that will fix everything. The people who don't have money are those who worry about not having money. The Universe gives us *exactly* what we think and expect about money. If we worry that we will never have enough, we won't have enough. Worrying over money is having a "poverty consciousness." It's as if you are putting a wall up in front of you, and that wall keeps money out of reach instead of letting it come to you.

Financial freedom is possible, but it may be a difficult thing to achieve. You have to really change your thinking about money. You have to rethink your poverty mentality. If you practice the idea that there is money for everyone, you can achieve financial abundance. In the meantime, here are some practical ways to let go of making money an issue in your life:

Set up a financial survival plan and determine your priorities for how you spend your money. Once that's done, don't obsess about it. Remember, true security and well-being come not from what we own, but who we are and the love we give and receive in our lives.

Create a budget. Do you know how much you actually spend each month? Happiness means living within your means. You do have control over the money you spend.

Don't be impulsive when you shop. Wait to buy something, making sure that it is something you really need. Eliminate buying things that are really unnecessary.

Stop thinking you need things to be happy.

Stop being envious of those you assume have something better than you do. Enjoy what you have.

Consolidate your debts and leave your credit cards at home.

How you handle money is a karmic lesson. The Universe gives you back what you give out. When you release your tight grip on money and use it to help others, you open up the flow and exchange of energy.

A friend of mine once told me a parable that truly depicts how greed and selfish beliefs about money can block our soul's development. I tell this tale in all my workshops and would like to share it with you:

A billionaire dies and goes to heaven. St. Peter stands at the Pearly Gates to greet him and show him around. As he walks through the heavenly environment with St. Peter, the billionaire is in awe of the celestial beauty and perfection. The gardens are impeccably manicured and filled with every imaginable exotic plant. Great mansions are aesthetically interspersed throughout the gardens. The beauty and majesty of heaven practically bring tears to the man's eyes. St. Peter continues guiding the man down a path. The surrounding colors are just incredible.

The man turns to St. Peter and asks, "Where is my house?"

St. Peter replies, "A little bit farther."

They walk down some steps. Suddenly, the man notices that the environment begins to change. The mansions are no longer mansions. They are cottages. The gardens are few and far between. The colors are lifeless and dull.

"Where is my home?" the man asks with some agitation.

"Just a few more steps," St. Peter responds.

They walk down several more steps and make a turn. By now, the atmosphere has altered completely. The houses are practically shacks; the colors have turned to gray and brown; the walkway is muddy, and the bountiful plant life has vanished.

Surprised at such a change, the man grabs St. Peter's arm. "Wait a minute. My house can't be here. You must have taken the wrong turn."

"No. This is correct," replies St. Peter.

They walk a little farther, and finally St. Peter stops. He points to a tiny hovel, barely standing upright. There are no plants, no colors, and no beauty. In fact, it is so dim, the man can hardly see.

The man turns to St. Peter and says, "You obviously don't know who I am. This can't be my house. On earth I had a great fortune. I owned ten homes and had hundreds of servants. I could buy whatever I wanted. I know this is some kind of mistake."

By this time, the man is huffing and puffing his protestation. "Whom can I speak to?"

St. Peter looks into the man's eyes and says, "There is no mistake. We could only build with the materials you sent us!"

The spiritual world does not reward the acquisition of money. In fact, money is regarded in a very different light; it is seen not as an end in itself, but as an instrument to assist others.

HAVING IT ALL

The following is a reading for a husband and wife who were extremely rich in the material sense, but bankrupt in the spiritual sense.

I was doing a demonstration in Orange County, and I noticed that many of the women who showed up were not my usual kind of audience. They were dressed to the nines, wore lots of jewelry, and had their hair and nails done, as if they had just come from the Ritz-Carlton Hotel.

I asked my assistant, "Is there some organization here today?"

My assistant knew exactly what I meant. "No," she said, "just a lot of rich women from La Jolla and Newport."

Midway during the demonstration, I saw a male spirit standing by one of the women in the audience. I could see he was anxious to get a message through.

I moved to the woman in the front row. She was wearing what looked like a tailored Chanel suit. Her hair, dark with golden highlights, and makeup that looked as if it had been professionally done that morning.

"May I come to you?" I asked the lovely woman.

"Yes, of course."

"There is a man here. He is anxious to speak to you. He says his name is Clifford or Clifton? Do you know who this is?"

"Yes, Cliff, my husband. He passed a few years ago."

"He seems to be upset about something. He is telling me that you need to change what you are doing."

"I don't know what that means," she replied.

I asked the spirit to clarify his message. I listened and talked to him while the audience waited with bated breath.

"Cliff says that he was wrong. He didn't know it until he got there. He is showing me a courtroom. Now I see a mansion. Does this make sense?"

"Yes. My husband was an attorney, and he had a very lucrative practice. We lived in a mansion in Newport. He was a workaholic."

"Please don't tell me anything more." Then I listened to Cliff again.

"Now he is showing me jewelry, champagne, boats, cars, and stacks and stacks of money. Who is Betty?"

"Betsy. That's me."

"He is saying that none of this matters. He is saying that when he got to the other side, he wasn't happy. I feel a lot of stuff around the head. A lot of confusion."

"That doesn't sound like Cliff. He always knew what he was doing."

"Well," I replied, "he doesn't have any control over his life in the spirit world. He is saying that he cheated people when he was alive. He is sorry that he lied. He was all wrapped up in the material world."

"Aren't we all?" Betsy said with a smirk.

"Who's Derek?"

"Our son. He died too."

I could hear the people in the audience whispering to one another. Betsy's eyes welled up with tears.

"Cliff is trying to convince you that you have to change. He took money from his clients. He overcharged them. He wants you to give away the money to those who need it. He says the money is blood money. He cheated people to get it. He wants you to set up a charity and donate his money."

Betsy looked dumbfounded and somewhat embarrassed. "I don't know what to say."

I could see that this woman didn't really hear what Cliff was trying to tell her. She was too wrapped up in her lifestyle.

"He is showing me a small plane. Did your husband and son die in a plane crash?"

"Yes, they died in Cliff's jet. He was teaching Derek how to fly."

"Cliff is down on his knees. He is begging you. He is saying, *Don't do what I did*. He says he made mistakes, and he is so unhappy that he took advantage of others."

Betsy seemed to be moved, but I could see that this was not what she wanted to hear. "Is my son around?" she asked.

"No. I am not getting anyone other than your husband."

"Okay. Well, tell Cliff that I'll think about the charity."

"You know you can talk to him yourself. He is always around."

"Oh, I hope not. I don't want him hanging around me all the time."

"He'll be there only when you want him," I said. Then I turned from Betsy and went on with the rest of the readings.

As with many of my demonstrations, people often write me years after their readings. Betsy was no exception.

Dear James,

You read for me at one of your appearances in Orange County. My name is Betsy and my husband Cliff came through that evening. I was unhappy at the time, and didn't want to listen to Cliff's advice. I was very caught up in my house, car, clothes, and material possessions. It was one way to soothe the pain of losing both Cliff and Derek, my son. I kept spending Cliff's money like it was growing on trees. I met a man and married him. He was just like me. He liked the good life. I learned a good lesson from him, because he swindled me out of my inheritance and left the country. I am now living in a small apartment and work in a department store. I should have listened to Cliff and started a charity. At least I would have spent the money on a good cause. I wanted to thank you for that night. I speak to Cliff all the time now. It was a costly price to pay, but I think I get it now.

Yours truly,
Betsy

Self-Esteem

Perhaps if Betsy had had more self-esteem, she would have understood that spending money on things would never make her whole inside. Lack of self-esteem is one of the biggest obstacles to overcome.

However, once you have mastered this lesson, the world is your playground and you can conquer anything. *Everything* in life stems from the perception you have of yourself. Measuring self-esteem is easy. Self-esteem is the difference between success and failure. If you have high self-esteem, you value yourself as worthy, and you feel that you can accomplish what you desire. If it is low, then you place very little value on yourself and feel like a loser.

I believe we come into this world with a certain set of values and a certain sense of self. I also believe that those to whom we look for guidance as we form our lives are extremely influential in making or breaking our self-esteem. When I was a young child, I had very few friends; the ones I had were never close. Because I always felt different, I never quite felt as if I fit in. In a sense, I felt alone.

One magical day, I was walking down the street in my neighbor-hood, and a car stopped beside me. A woman rolled down her window and called to me. She said she was a new neighbor around the block and asked me to come over to her house and play with her son. We were the same age. That night, I went over to her house and met her son Scott. He and I became best friends, but it was Scott's mother, Connie, who had the greatest effect on my life. She would always en-courage me by saying how wonderful I was: "Don't you dare ever listen to anyone who picks on you, because they don't see how special you are!"

Connie's insight, encouragement, and unconditional love helped to instill confidence in me, which was always there but was never realized. I can honestly say that if it wasn't for Connie Leif, I would not be where I am today, and you would not be reading this book.

What is the easiest way to build self-esteem or, as I like to say, remind yourself how great you are?

Reevaluate how you look at yourself. Do you make predominantly self-defeating judgments about yourself? Realize that you are falli-ble and imperfect, like everyone else. Don't beat yourself up when you make a mistake or a choice that doesn't turn out the way you want.

Scrutinize your actions. Are you harming or helping others? Many times we give others more respect and more leeway than we give ourselves.

Become your own caregiver and compassionate observer.

Don't look at yourself in parts, for example, as having a nice smile or a nice body. See yourself as a whole being made up of wonderful intricacies and traits.

Be flexible in your attitude. Forgive your flaws and the flaws of others. We are all learning to be and do the best we can.

Give everyone who crosses your path the benefit of the doubt.

Make a list of the wonderful aspects that you love about your being. Put those good qualities into practice with one person at a time and notice how your love and goodness can help to change another.

Distractions

Today's hectic life is full of distractions. We are plugged into cell phones, BlackBerrys, and Bluetooth. Everything is in hyperspeed, and multitasking is the order of the day. Distractions can be damaging to our sense of worth, because they take away our focus. We cannot accomplish what we wish, and we end up stressed out. Distractions consume a lot of mental energy that is better applied elsewhere. My good friend Joerdie once told me to write down the word "Distractions" on a piece of paper and place it wherever I can see it. I stuck it on my refrigerator, so I was sure to see it every day. Guess what? It works! Whenever I see it, it reminds me of my priorities, and I don't let the distractions take me away from what's important.

There are many sources of distractions, internal as well as external:

Family, friends, and co-workers who don't nourish you.

Television, radio, and DVR's.

Cell phones and text messaging.

Video games.

Computers and e-mail.

Leaf blowers and barking dogs.

Gossip.

Self-critical inner chatter.

Not living up to others people's expectations.

Procrastination.

How can you deal with these distractions? Coping with distractions and minor irritations is mainly a matter of attitude. You can either dwell on them and blow them out of proportion, or you can accept them and go on with your life.

Addictions

Addiction is probably one of the most common and potentially destructive obstacles facing most people today. Although the term "addiction" is usually used with reference to drugs or alcohol, it covers much more territory than that. It is fair to say that most of us possess at least *some* kind of addiction. The definition of addiction is: an obsession, a recurring compulsion, or an excessive physiological or psychological dependence.

If we are physiologically addicted, we are dependent on some substance such as medicine, illegal drugs, or alcohol. If we stop taking the chemical, a withdrawal process occurs in the body. A psychological addiction causes us to perform behavior that may give us a quick fix in order to decrease anxiety and stress. Psychological addictions include compulsive gambling, sex, eating, shopping, Internet surfing, working, and playing of video games. Like distractions, they can sabotage our sense of self. These behaviors may not have physiological manifestations, but they can be just as devastating as substance dependence.

Many factors influence the development of addictions. Some are inherited; others may stem from unresolved childhood issues, including family dysfunction, abuse, and emotional stress, causing certain escapist behaviors. A lack of self-esteem contributes to addictive behavior, as people always look outside themselves to fill the void left by the lack of self-love.

It may be that people with these behaviors are overly sensitive or overly emotional and get hurt easily. They escape by placing themselves in an altered state of consciousness, because they can't or won't function in day-to-day situations. Instead, they shut off their pain and refuse to feel anymore. They receive gratification only from addictive behavior and will do anything to reexperience it. If these individuals only knew that something as simple as meditation can help! Meditation not only brings one to higher states of consciousness, but promotes a sense of oneness, peace of mind, and well-being, expands perception, and allows one to see the fullness in all things!

How can addictions be treated? That depends on the severity of the addiction and the particular addiction itself. Generally speaking, treatment needs to be for the whole being: body, mind, and spirit. First and foremost, addicted persons need to have the desire to get better and off whatever they are addicted to. Second, they must explore exactly why this behavior has developed in their lives. Then, a strong support system definitely needs to be in place. It helps if the support is in part comprised of individuals who have gone through the same type of experience. Psychological counseling is a definite must and, I believe, a key to a successful recovery.

A TRIPLE WHAMMY

I remember the next situation quite vividly. A few years back, I was hosting a demonstration as part of a weekend of seminars by different guest lecturers. There were two young women in the audience who caught my eye right away. A female spirit stood to the side of them, and she looked as if she was counting. I thought it was amusing, so I went over to the two women.

"What are your names, please?" I asked.

Caught by surprise, they responded, "I'm Deborah, and this is my sister, Barbara."

I closed my eyes to get a sense of their energy. Then I looked again at the spirit standing next to them. She was still counting. I could tell she wasn't paying attention to me.

"I have to tell you that there is an older woman standing right by the two of you, and she is oblivious to what is going on here. She looks like she is counting. Does this make any sense to you?"

The two girls looked at one another, and their jaws dropped.

"It must be Mom!" exclaimed Deborah.

"Why is she counting?" I asked.

"She's a hoarder, or was," said Barbara. "Our house used to be stacked high from floor to ceiling with everything and anything you can imagine. She used to count her things to make sure neither of us threw anything out."

I was flabbergasted. "Oh my God. Well, she's still counting," I said with a grin on my face.

Deborah said, "She kicked us out of the house and, frankly, we were glad to leave. We couldn't stand living in that house of horrors. There were narrow paths everywhere just wide enough to walk from one room to another. We were so embarrassed. All our friends would whisper behind our backs about our mother being a nut job."

I received many impressions from the girls' mother. "Is her name Ann or Anna?"

"Annemarie."

I felt a little dizzy for a second and put my hand to my head. "Was she a drinker? I get the feeling of being woozy from your mother."

"She was an alcoholic. She used to count the bottles of vodka even when they were empty. And a smoker too. She was a heavy smoker."

"Three addictions!" I said with surprise.

Annemarie stopped counting and looked at me. She sent me her thoughts. *Yes, I can hear you,* I telepathically replied. Then she moved to where her daughters were sitting and gave them each a hug.

"Your mother recognizes that you are here. She is talking about the jewelry. Are you wearing her jewelry? She is telling me that it's her necklace and her rings."

"Yes, I am wearing one of her rings," Barbara interjected. "Is she okay?"

"Your mother is saying that she took her addictions with her when she passed. She knows now how bad it was for you. She was so caught up in hoarding especially, and then the drinking and smoking. Her mind was poisoned in a way, and she became a prisoner in her own home."

"Is she still addicted to those things there?" asked Barbara.

"No. She says she is part of a therapy group. She is saying that at the beginning she spent her days in a lower, dark, and scary existence. She was with people like herself. A lot of drunks. She has been with others who suffer from earthly addictions. They are working them out there."

"We didn't get a chance to say good-bye before she died. We had a really big fight about the house. We tried to get it condemned as a fire hazard. Between her hoarding, smoking, and drinking, we thought we'd all go up in flames. She got so mad at us. We really feel bad about that," Barbara said as tears welled up in her eyes.

"Yes. We want to tell her we still love her, no matter what," said Deborah.

"Your mother is sorry for what she put you through. She says that she misses your father. He is somewhere else. Your father liked to study, and he is at peace now. She misses seeing him."

Then I got some more impressions from Annemarie. "Your mother says that she felt so much freer when she finally let go. She is part of a group—I guess you would call them spirit guides. They move around the earthly plane and work with young people in bars and clubs, trying to influence them to give up smoking and drinking."

"Good for you, Mom," Deborah and Barbara chimed in simultaneously.

Addictions often come up in my readings. There are so many people "hooked" on something. The spirit world has said that this earth is the land of addictions, and one of the reasons many of us choose to come back to this earth is to work out our addictive behavior. It is also very true that spirits are persistent about our curing our addictions while on the earthly plane; otherwise we bring these addictions to the spirit world, as Annemarie did. We cannot make progress in spirit while our minds are still fixated on earthly addictions. Eventually, the addictive desire will burn out in spirit, but if handled on earth, it will be one less item of unfinished business to hold on to.

EIGHT

Taking the High Road

The learner always begins by finding fault, but the scholar sees the positive merit in everything.

—Georg Wilhelm Hegel

T ake the high road" was a phrase I had heard one Sunday morning in 1986 from Manly Palmer Hall at his lecture at the Philosophical Research Society in Los Angeles. Mr. Hall was one of the great New Thought philosophers of the twentieth century. He wrote hundreds of books on spirituality, most of which are considered classics in the New Age community. When I heard him speak that morning, it was almost as if a friend handed me a key to the door of rightful perspective. His words have helped me avoid getting caught up in the small stuff of the ego that matters little in the grand scheme of things.

This idea came up again when I was sharing a lovely dinner one night recently at a restaurant on the famous Melrose Avenue in Los Angeles. My close friend Lisa, who I really think is an angel in disguise, and I were discussing life, one of our favorite subjects. Whether over the phone or in person, the two of us often spend hours philoso-phizing about life, death, and the reasons why people choose to behave the way they do. This particular evening, I mentioned how upset I had been with the people in the Hollywood community.

"They have no respect or awareness," I commented. "They will exploit anyone for a dollar." It really saddened me.

Lisa looked at me with a twinkle in her eye and said, "Always take the high road, James. There is less traffic up there."

She was right. I knew that whatever bothered me about Hollywood was trivial. It was my ego that got bruised. I was just annoyed that others were not aware of their spiritual responsibility.

All of us get frustrated about what we cannot control or when it appears as though others are using us for their gain. If we could look at these situations in a different light, we would definitely be less frus-trated along life's path. It can be extremely difficult for us to focus on the good when bad things occur in our lives, but if we could pay atten-tion to our truth and purpose, our lives would flow more easily. In the long run, we would become healthier, more productive, and more spir-itually minded human beings.

So how do we retrain ourselves to take the high road? First, we have to find out what keeps us from traveling the high road. I suggest you take a moment, go to a quiet place where you will not be disturbed, and take a look at your recent reactions to life situations.

Are you immediately negative? Negative thinking limits your per-spective. Do you have a pessimistic attitude? "He will never like me. I am not good-looking enough." "Who cares what they think? They're just stupid anyway." Do you recognize your destructive way of think-ing? Do you see that there can be a positive way to deal with situa-tions?

Do you tend to make assumptions and draw conclusions without evidence to back them up? Don't make your mind up before you have all of the information about a situation. There is a wonderful saying:

"To ass-u-me is to make an ass out of you and me." Before you jump to conclusions, take a moment to stop and step back from the situation at hand. Take a few deep breaths and ask yourself: "What is the higher good here?" There can be a multitude of reasons why something appears a certain way, and the truth may not be outwardly apparent.

Do you limit your world because of low self-esteem and self-worth? If you think, "I'll never get married. Who would want me?" or "I'll never have money in the future," you are creating that particular limited situation in your life.

Are you carrying a chip on your shoulder? Do you say to yourself, "Nothing good will ever happen to me"? This type of thinking cuts you off from life's possibilities. If you feel like a victim, you have already halted the magic. Your life will reflect your stagnant narrow-mindedness. As I have said previously, and will throughout the book, fear is limiting and love is limitless.

Another way to avoid the high road is through hubris. When you think that everyone around you is wrong and only you have the right answer, your arrogance blocks the flow of intuition and energy. You have, in essence, put on blinders. You will miss so much of life this way.

Only you are responsible for how you react to a situation. Thinking positively, giving the other person the benefit of the doubt, opens the door to miracles. Situations, relationships, jobs, money, you name it, will unfold in the most uncanny ways—ways you would not expect. When you take charge of your thoughts, you are, in essence, taking the high road.

AN OPEN MIND IS AN OPEN HEART

It is extremely difficult for me to give a message from the spirit world to someone whose thinking is negative and limited, because spirit is expansive. In order for spirits to reach us, our minds must be open to what could be. Negative thinking, skepticism, and control create restriction, and spirits cannot harness the energy from us necessary to communicate. The following example shows how destructive thinking and skepticism closed down the channels to a daughter's desperate plea for love.

Toward the end of my presentation in front of an audience in New York, a female spirit of about thirty years old came through.

"There is a young woman here, and she gives me the initials J. T. Does this spirit belong to anyone here?"

After five painstaking minutes, a man raised his hand and pointed to the man next to him.

"Those are his initials."

I walked toward the man who seemed resistant to participate. "May I come to you, please?"

"I don't really believe in this stuff," he replied. Pointing to the man on his left, he said, "It's all his idea. He dragged me here."

I've heard this remark more times than I care to remember. Nevertheless, I continued. "What is your name?"

"Jake."

"Jake, there is a woman here who is standing right next to you. She is showing me a hospital. She died in St. Vincent's Hospital. Is this correct?"

"I really don't know what you're talking about."

I could tell Jake didn't want to talk to this spirit and had some problem with her.

"She is showing me blood, and some dark spots in the blood. Did she have cancer?"

Jake didn't believe it was real. He responded, "I really don't want to do this."

I knew he knew the spirit, but he didn't want to own up to it. He was really closed off, and encouraging him to participate felt like pulling teeth.

"You are very shut down," I said. "It's really hard for me to connect with the spirit world when you close off your energy. She has a lot to share with you, but you are not giving her the chance."

People in the audience were turning to look at Jake. I could tell they were frustrated too. I felt that they wanted me to move on and help someone else who *wanted* to communicate with a lost loved one.

"You know, Jake, this woman wants to tell you things, but if you are not open to her, I can't force you."

"I'm sorry, but I just don't believe in this stuff. If this spirit, as you say, wants to talk to me, why didn't she talk to me when she was alive?"

"Is this your daughter?" I asked with surprise.

Jake didn't answer. I could hear people in the audience groan their dissatisfaction.

"Your daughter is telling me she was in the hospital for a long time. She tried to call you, but you wouldn't answer. Did the two of you have a fight?"

Jake really didn't want to participate in the reading, and he sat there stoically. Although it was difficult for me, the spirit was persistent. "Will you at least admit that this spirit is your daughter?"

The man next to Jake finally answered for his friend. "Yes, Cecilia was his daughter. She died of leukemia last year."

At least it was some response. The spirit used Jake's friend's energy. "You fought with Cecilia about her husband, didn't you?"

Jake sat there quietly; he did not answer. His friend nodded affirmatively.

"Cecilia is telling me that you were angry at her because her husband was Muslim and you didn't want her to marry him."

The audience buzzed.

Jake admitted, "I didn't like him, but not because he was a Muslim."

"Your daughter is trying to tell you that she forgives you. She is kneeling and crying. Do you want to say something to her?"

Jake refused to admit anything else. I felt sorry for the spirit, but I am only the conduit. I can't make people do anything.

I turned to Jake and said, "Why don't you accept your daughter's message?"

Jake would not respond.

At that point, a spirit guide appeared. It was a beautiful woman in a colorful Japanese kimono tied with a sash. She wrapped her arms around Cecilia, and they disappeared together. I went on to another guest.

At the end of the event, I was in the back of the auditorium signing books. Jake's friend handed me a book to sign. He shrugged. "What can I say? Jake's a hard nut to crack." We both smiled.

Several months later I received an e-mail from Jake on my Web site. He apologized for his behavior and for not being more forthcoming. He said that he was afraid to admit he was wrong in front of such a big crowd, but he wanted to thank me for communicating his daughter's message.

It is important to realize that when your thinking pattern is emotionally based, like Jake's, you're not able to perceive things honestly as they actually are. Jake responded to his emotion instead of the reality of the situation. Instead of acknowledging his daughter, he stayed stuck in the thought, "I don't feel happy about this." Not only was Jake biased against a certain ethnic culture; he was also too proud to admit that he might have made a mistake about his daughter's husband.

One of the hardest things to learn is that you cannot control other people's actions or motivations. I certainly felt frustrated with Jake because of his stubbornness, yet there was nothing I could do to change his mind. Ironically, in some ways the best aspects of my work are also my worst. Being sensitive, I am overly aware of people who are not being honest and forthright. Judging these people is an easy way out, but is not the way to go. They are who they are, and I cannot control them. So many people write to me and speak to me of their frustration with loved ones who don't believe in this work or life after death. I tell them, as I tell myself, their reality is their reality. Skeptics think that they are doing the right thing, and if they don't have much awareness and sensitivity, they might be. I must see it for what it is and realize that I am only responsible for my own steps on this earth.

A GENTLE SOUL

One of the most enlightening insights I have discovered through my mediumship came as a total surprise. It put to rest the belief that when you're dead you have complete knowledge and awareness of the Universe. This idea could not be farther from the truth. Many spirits have shared that they continually learn new things, especially by observing their loved ones on earth. Spirits are always watching our reactions to various life situations and acquiring new knowledge.

While writing this book, I was asked to give a demonstration at an event at a Reno resort. This was my first time in such a setting, so I was a bit skeptical. I remember my very first steps as I walked into the casino. I was knocked over not only by the wafting smoke escaping through the open door, but also by the number of earthbound spirits who were hanging out and attaching themselves to unaware hosts who kept pushing buttons on the slot machines. I immediately felt like a stranger in a strange land. I thought, "There is no way I can work here." The energy of this polluted psychic atmosphere would render it almost impossible to expand the consciousness of this crowd. However, the response I received at the event was even more mind-boggling. The audience was so receptive and so appreciative of my coming all the way to their part of the world that they hung on every word that came out of my mouth. Because they were so thrilled, to say the least, I was very humbled by their heartfelt reaction.

At the start, I was attracted to a spirit who seemed to be new to the spirit world. I could tell because when I tuned into him, he felt as

though he had just passed. Then he quickly said to me, *I am new here.*
He was standing beside a man with long gray sideburns and a ponytail
who was sitting on the far left of the auditorium.

I walked to the spot and asked. "Is your name Mason?"

The man stood up. "Yes, I'm Mason. You can call me Mace."

"I have your brother here. He seems new to the spirit world. Did
he die recently?"

"Yes. He died five months ago," Mace responded.

"Your brother is describing his funeral. He was happy to see all his
friends there. He is telling me that there were many family members
who met him."

"Yeah, we come from a pretty big family. I'm glad to hear they were
there to meet him."

"I'm getting the initial P."

"My brother Peter," Mace replied.

"Peter is thanking you for teaching him how to deal with people."

"Pete never was one to give someone else the benefit of the doubt."

"You taught him how to be kind and considerate when he wouldn't
otherwise have been. He wasn't one to show compassion to others."

"Yeah. He was pretty tough on people."

"There is a whole group of people here now." I listened to the
group. "They're telling me that they played bridge. You don't strike me
as someone who plays bridge."

"Yeah. I might look a bit scuzzy, but looks are deceiving."

"You're right. Your friends can feel your love, so they come and
visit you a lot."

"Great! Tell them I miss them."

"They hear you, Mace. One of them is telling me that you are very
spiritual, but not in a religious way."

"No, I'm not very religious. I know people have a lot of different
beliefs, so I try to give them some slack. No reason to judge them."

"They are thanking you. They learned a lot from you about people. They can see how they judged people while you did not."

"Thanks, guys." Mace was a bit flustered.

"Keep doing the good work," I said to Mace. Then I moved on to others.

As you can see, Mace's positive outlook, compassion, and lack of negative judgment taught others to be friendly instead of being small-minded and critical of others.

Change Your Thinking

Once you have evaluated your negative ways of thinking, it is time to begin the work of replacing negatives with positives. For example, "I am not good enough" can be changed to "I am better each day." Replace the thought "I don't have the money" with "I have a limitless supply of money." You must think positively in every aspect of your life in order to attract positive things to you. Make a choice to find the good in everything, and you will create a much more positive life for yourself.

As with everything in life, changing your thoughts is a process. Because it is a new practice for you, be patient; change will not happen overnight. Think of it as a game. See how many times you catch yourself with a negative thought and replace it with a positive one. After about a month of consciously working at this, you will definitely notice an improvement. Positive attracts more positive. I recommend a wonderful book to all my students to help shift negative to more positive thinking called *The Game of Life and How to Play It* by Florence Scovel Shinn. Written in 1925, during the New Thought awakening, the book still rings true—in fact, it may even be more applicable today.

Many years ago, I began a conscious effort to rid myself of negative thoughts and all negativity in my life. The first thing I noticed was that friends with whom I had been close for a number of years vanished from my life, and positive, more loving individuals soon replaced them. When you start changing your thoughts to positive supportive ones, every aspect of your life shifts. As you continue to change your thinking, set some goals for yourself. Be as specific as you possibly can. No matter how outrageous an idea, if you want it, send out the thought and own it. See your goal as if it has already happened.

As I began to think more positively, I decided it was a good time to make just such a goal list for myself. I lived in LA at the time and decided to get out of town, so I could think more clearly. I went to the bus station in Santa Monica and boarded a bus headed for Santa Barbara. On the drive up, I sat back and relaxed, admiring the scenery along the coast highway. Upon my arrival I went into a stationery store and bought a blank journal. Then I walked down to the beach, found a rock to sit on, rejoiced in the beauty of the scenery, and began to jot down a list of goals I wanted to accomplish within the next fifteen years. One of them was to be a *New York Times* best-selling author and touch the rest of the world with my teachings. Another was to own my own house. Both of these goals materialized (plus about eight more goals) within the following fifteen years. The thing to remember is to be positive and open. Don't try to control how the Universe will bring your goals to you. Just let go and let God, knowing all shall be given to you in divine, right time.

Say You're Sorry

Being conscious of your thinking patterns and ridding negativity from your thoughts and life are the basics for taking the high road. However, if you hold on to bitterness and are unwilling to forgive and apologize, you are building your foundation on sand. In order to bask in the splendors that await you, you must heal unresolved feelings and unspoken sorrows. You must learn to apologize.

A key to getting along well with people is knowing when to say you're sorry. Personally, I have found that occasionally when I have said something half-heartedly, someone misunderstood my comment and was offended. You never know how someone else will respond to what you do or what emotions will be triggered by what you say. Little things can add up. People hold grudges, and grudges grow into conflicts. If it is obvious that you have offended someone, apologize right away. I have done this many times, because I don't want anyone to have any misunderstandings.

How can you tell the areas in your life where an apology may be in order? This will take another type of evaluation:

Do you have a difficult time sustaining a relationship due to trust issues?

Do friends or family members call you less frequently than they used to?

Do you dwell on past offenses?

Do you have angry outbursts at the smallest things?

Do you ever get the sense that you are not being heard or that no one fully understands you?

Do you find that you drink or take drugs to escape confrontation?

Do you feel your life has lost its purpose?

If you said yes to any of the questions above, there may be people you need to apologize to. You might ask some of them if they were offended by something you said. Sometimes a person will blow it off, saying, "I'm okay," but then several months go by, and the same person hasn't wanted anything to do with you. The person was not honest with you and obviously didn't have the courage to tell you the truth. This is a difficult position, but others have their reasons, and you can only do so much. Just be true to yourself and make an effort to mend broken fences.

Make a list of people you feel need an apology—those who resent you or are holding a grudge against you. After making the list, write next to each name the offense that occurred and the reason to apologize. If you are unsure if an apology is in order, ask the person if there was a problem between the two of you and see if there is a way to clear up the misunderstanding.

Apologizing is not an easy thing to do. Many of us feel ashamed to admit that we have hurt or wronged someone. Sometimes our pride can get in the way of an apology, and we are not sure how to go about it. I have put together some tips on how to start.

First, you must admit to yourself that you have offended someone. It may not be obvious to you. Perhaps you need to see how other people react to you. The important thing is to take responsibility for your offense.

Make sure your apology is genuine and comes from the heart. People will be able to sense if you truly mean what you say. It's important to explain that you didn't mean to offend. You must show that you take it seriously and recognize that your actions created a problem for another person.

Show your regret. Don't start justifying your actions, or the apology will not seem sincere. The other person needs to know that you have genuinely suffered by your actions and that you are sorry.

You also must make it known that you are willing to change and repair the damage you have caused. For instance, if you made some verbal comments that offended someone, you can say that you will be very mindful of what comes out of your mouth in the future.

Last, be prepared for the fact that your apology may not be accepted. It does not matter. The most important thing is that you spoke your truth, and you were genuine in your words and feelings. You cannot control how another person reacts. You will have to let it go. Again, no one can control other persons or their feelings.

There are ways to apologize to others if you feel as though you can't confront them in person. Try different methods to see which might be more effective in touching their heart.

Call them on the telephone. Some people feel much more comfortable when not face-to-face. Most apologies work on the phone, because there is distance between you and the other person. Of course, this method is necessary when you are in a different city, but it is also recommended if you feel there could be a chance of violence or abusive behavior as a response.

Another method I tell *all* of my clients to do is to sit down and write either a card or a letter to express apologetic feelings. Because the other person knows you actually went to the trouble of sitting down, thinking about it, and then writing about it, there is a greater chance that he or she will accept the apology and realize you are sincere. Remember, what you say will be on paper and be around for a long time; it may even be read by other people. This is okay, because if others read it, it shows them that you took responsibility for your actions and that you took the high road.

Admitting you are wrong and apologizing go a long way in your development as a spiritual human being. I cannot tell you how powerful an effect they have on the living and the dead.

THE LETTER

The following occurred some years back when I was still doing private readings. A young man, Jeffrey Slazak, came for his appointment at my home in West Hollywood. At first he seemed quite distraught, and I hoped that spirits would be able to get through.

After our initial greetings, he said, "I am really anxious for some advice."

After my preliminary prayer, I immediately saw a woman standing behind his right shoulder. I knew this must be his mother.

"Jeffrey, there is a woman here. I think she is your mother. Her name is strange, sounds like a man's name. Robert, Rob, something like that."

"Roberta, but everyone called her Bobbi."

"Your mother is with her mother and father, your grandparents. She seems upset about something and is so glad that you came here today."

"I could feel her around me all morning. That's probably why I am so anxious."

"She is saying that she left the earth still holding a grudge against her sister who she thinks was jealous of her."

"Yes. Exactly! Of course, I was on my mother's side. I haven't spoken to my aunt or uncle, even my cousins, since my mother's passing."

"Your mother is saying that she was wrong. She made a terrible mistake. She wants you to make amends for her, since she cannot."

Jeffrey hesitated. "I'm not in a good place right now. I don't know if I can face my aunt and uncle. Tell her I'll try, but I'm not promising."

"I know it's hard to apologize, especially since you're not really the one who had the fight in the first place. But your mother is begging. She wants you to write a letter and tell your aunt how sorry she is. She is saying that writing would be easier for you. Until there is an apology, she cannot move from where she is in spirit. She is telling me that she is stuck on a level and cannot move up till this healing takes place."

Jeffrey shook his head. "Okay, I'll think about it."

I continued the reading for another twenty minutes. Jeffrey's mother and grandparents expressed their love for him. By the time Jeffrey left, he felt much calmer.

"Thank you, James. I feel better. I hope I am up to the task."

A year later, I met Penny, the person who recommended that Jeffrey come and see me.

"You did wonders for Jeffrey," Penny said. "He was so moved by the information you gave him, especially the things his mother said about his aunt. He wrote his aunt a letter and apologized for his mother and himself. The letter came back to him unopened. Several months later, he was driving to the store, and a stray dog ran in front of his truck. He was able to stop in time. He called the number on the dog's collar, and who do you think it belonged to?"

By now I was utterly fascinated. "Who?" I asked impatiently.

"The dog belonged to his aunt's daughter."

"You're kidding," I exclaimed.

"Wait! There's more," Penny continued. "When he went to return the dog, his aunt was there. They were having a birthday party."

"Amazing."

"Jeffrey was able to explain about the letter he wrote. His aunt said that she never got it. She told Jeffrey how upset she was about how she had left things with Bobbi. She told him that she wanted to make things right again. He told them about you. His aunt was so happy to learn about her sister."

"I'm so glad to hear that. Now Bobbi can move on."

"One more thing," Penny added. "Jeffrey had been unemployed for six months. His aunt asked him how he was doing, and he told her. She said she knew someone who was looking for an employee and set him up with a job."

We can all transform ourselves. Beautiful things happen when we apologize, forgive, and take the high road. That is when healing truly begins. Do something "high road" today. Start by opening a door or holding an elevator for someone. Thank your waiter, the bus driver, or the cabbie, even when you don't want to. Begin raising your consciousness and find God in everyone you meet. The closer you come to recognizing and connecting to the Higher Self of other people, the closer you are to understanding their true spiritual nature. And as a result, everyone's path becomes clearer and easier to walk.

NINE

Clarity of Consciousness

*Life is a process of becoming, a combination of
states we have to go through. Where people fail
is that they wish to elect a state and remain in
it. This is a kind of death.*

—Anaïs Nin

It had been several weeks, and work on the dream I was exploring
had come to a standstill. I could not retain anything that even re-
motely bore any connection to the dream. Then after two days of
constantly asking the Universe to please give me closure about this
dream, it happened! At four o'clock the next morning, I had just returned to my bed after using the bathroom, and I fell into a deep, deep
sleep. I distinctly remember the familiar feeling I had experienced
whenever this particular dream came into my sleeping consciousness.
I found myself staring at several oil paintings of flowers, then one of a
landscape, and then another of a California hillside. I knew these
paintings! I had seen them before. But, where? I then recalled these
were the exact same images that appeared in the dream weeks before.

In that very first encounter, I had seen them outside a hospital window. I felt myself being pulled to another location. Now I was at a yard sale, and the paintings were among various items for sale. I looked to the right and then to the left and saw some incredible pieces of art deco jewelry—bracelets, earrings, and an assortment of bangles and beads. They all looked so familiar, as if I had held them in my very own hands.

Then the shadows seemed to lift, and my moment of clarity had arrived. I looked around the yard and into the garage. Several people were milling about. A short woman with dark hair turned around and smiled at me. Her eyes were greener than I had remembered; her smile lit up the entire place. She glided right toward me and reached for my hand. "Oh, James!" she said. Before me stood my very dear friend who lived down the street. She had died several months earlier. The realism startled me so much that I shot up out of bed and exclaimed, "Violette!"

Anytime the death of someone we know occurs, it brings to our awareness the question of our own death and forces us to give serious consideration to who we are and where we are going. Violette's death had done just that to me.

What is life about? Who are you? How would you describe your personality traits, your education, employment, life experience, and the situation in which you currently live? Is that all of *you*? When you look in the mirror and see yourself staring back, you may think that is you. You can see the body with your mind, so obviously there is a mental element besides a physical one. You can intellectualize, rationalize, read, write, and make decisions. By being conscious of these abilities, you are even more than what you think. You are consciousness itself. You are conscious of being *aware*.

It is ironic that humans think that their departed loved ones are *dead*. In reality, our so-called dead relatives are more alive than we are on earth. Spirits are in a new level of consciousness, an awareness they did not take the time to acknowledge during their sojourn on earth. I have had thousands of spirits tell me, *You call us dead? Most of you are the walking dead! You have no sense of the world around or within you.*

All too often we go through life busying ourselves with things to do. In fact, many of us write "to do" lists. We are completely involved with doing, having, and making, instead of *being.* Our lives are a series of routines. We go to work, eat, earn money, and then return home, eat, and go to sleep. The next day the routine begins all over again.

Our minds are cluttered with other people's projections and judgments, most of which are fear-based. We give these projections and judgments such reality that most of us are living someone else's version of life. It's difficult to have a sense of who we are when we are living out our parents', spouse's, church's, and the media's conscious and unconscious projections.

Yes, we all want to be loved and please others. However, we shouldn't do this at the expense of our self-worth and self-awareness. We are willing to put ourselves down in order to fulfill the expectations and projections of other people. We worry about the past and the future, even though those two things don't really exist. Past and future are merely concepts. The only thing we have control over is the present. Life is made up of moments, and we are responsible for these moments. We can fill them with *stuff* or use them to be more aware of ourselves and the world in which we reside. We have to go beyond existing to *living.* When we take the time and devote ourselves to exploring who we truly are, we will open to the various levels of our consciousness. We will soon find we are much more than our physical appearance and physical lives, for the physical is merely the tip of the iceberg.

Spirits have talked incessantly about their biggest oversight while living on the earth. They did not realize that their physical bodies were simply housing for their souls and that their souls existed beyond their five senses. They want so much to help us to understand the value of *thought.* It is through our thoughts that the world can be filled with either magic or misery. Our thoughts direct everything in life. Think of thought as the conductor of our life's symphony. Do you want Mozart or a few notes of a forgettable song? It only takes moments a day to learn to use your mind in the correct way.

Another thing the spirits have realized on the spirit side of life is that the reality of God is very different from what they had been taught while on earth. Most of us have grown up with some form of belief in God; some of us haven't. Our religious belief systems are often subsumed under the all-encompassing label of "spirituality." To me, religion and spirituality are two very different and distinct concepts. A religious person is not necessarily spiritual, and a spiritual person is not necessarily religious. Spirituality is how one expresses one's *spirit*. Religion is a set of rules and limitations that are placed on an individual's spirit. The first is natural and infinite; the latter is a human construct and finite.

Depending on the spirit and the belief system it had while on earth, a myriad of interesting comments about God have been made: *I feel God everywhere. God is in everything we look at and everything we touch. I feel the presence of God with every person I meet here.* Spirits realize that God is not a person in a different geographic location, but an omnipresent energy, a consciousness that permeates everything and everyone.

Meditation and Prayer

In actuality, God is a formless multidimensional reality much like electromagnetic waves that pass through space. Imagine standing on a beach and watching the sun's rays dancing through the water illuminating the ocean floor. The multidimensional consciousness of God is like the sun through the water. Its energy permeates everything in and around us.

This multidimensionality operates through a range of frequencies or levels of reality. These realities are not above and below us, but inside us. The notions of above and below have to do with heaven and hell. As I have said in my workshops and books, heaven and hell are not above, below, or in any *place*. When seeking the highest levels of this multidimensional consciousness, we need to direct ourselves inward. This is where God resides.

No matter what name you apply to God, whether it is Jehovah, Allah, Ishvara, Tao, Great Spirit, or Jesus, in truth there is only the *formless One*. Those seeking God and desiring to have a relationship with God need only to go within to their hearts. How do we get to this inner world? As many sages have passed on, it is accomplished by quieting the mind in prayer and meditation.

Prayer is one of the greatest tools we possess. Through prayer, we can transcend the physical by connecting our minds to our hearts. We direct our thoughts and desires to the one force, the one source that is all of life. One does not need to be in a special building or perform a certain ritual to speak to God. God is anywhere and everywhere; God is limitless.

Prayer can take any form you choose. When you pray, simply acknowledge the truth that lies within your heart. It is not necessary to pray for oneself. By understanding that God resides in our hearts, we acknowledge that this consciousness already knows what we need. The more aware we are, the more we will realize that all things happen for a reason. Suffering, illness, disasters, hunger, plagues, viruses, and so on are lessons souls must learn as they journey on their divine path.

The optimum way to pray is selflessly. Praying for others creates good feelings inside us. It directs energy away from the egocentric self and redirects this energy to others. In giving to others, we truly give to ourselves. I often tell my audiences that when prayer is done with sincerity and humility, it is as if we are sending out pearls of unconditional love to others.

If you want to know what you are here to do, how you can be more loving, or how to get through a difficult situation, my answer is always *meditate.* The difference between prayer and meditation is that when we pray, we are asking for something, and when we meditate, we are listening to the answer. Meditation can be formal or informal. In formal meditation you follow a certain format, like sitting in a particular position, keeping your eyes closed, saying a mantra, and so forth. Free-flowing meditation has no requirements—you don't even have to close your eyes. Personally, I practice a little bit of both in my own way. Formally, I use a guided meditation—one that I have created over the years to bring me to my heart center. The other way I meditate is by watering the garden, making a flower arrangement, looking at the ocean, reading a book, or painting a picture. All meditation has one thing in common—quieting the busy mind.

The idea behind meditation is not necessarily that we force ourselves to have no distractions in our minds. Rather, we acknowledge the distractions and let them be what they are. Let's say that you sit cross-legged on a mat and formally meditate. There is a constant chatter in your head about life, the family, what you are going to have for dinner, or outside disturbances you hear like a lawn-mower motor or people talking. Acknowledge in your mind that these distractions exist and then let them go. The less you judge them and the less power you give them, the more you will be able to move into a relaxed state of being. At first this can be somewhat daunting, because it means giving up control. For those with compulsive behavior, distracting thought patterns, or emotional depression, control seems like the only security, the only thing to hold on to. In truth, trying to control the distractions holds them to us. The more we let go, the more we soar. In order to expand and reach new heights, we must not tie ourselves to the ground, or that's *all* we will see.

With an ongoing meditation practice, we will begin to see the bigger picture, and our places in that bigger picture. It also gives us greater control over our lives. We also begin to recognize the core of our being—the true self (as opposed to the ego self).

Meditation helps us to develop our multidimensional conscious-ness as well as recognize our connection to love. The more we medi-tate, the more we have a greater sense of God/Love. When we meditate, we clearly see what holds us back from that consciousness of love. We learn how the heavy energies of fear, greed, anger, jealousy, violence, self-indulgence, and envy tend to cut us off from truth and get in our way of living self-fulfilled lives—ones that we can be proud of.

Various levels of consciousness can be attained in meditation. Once we leave the confines of the egocentric state through deep contempla-tion, we are free to soar higher and realize that we are indeed part of a greater awareness and are in unity with all of it. This realization is cosmic consciousness. Perceiving the world from a higher perspective assists us in understanding our own path and the self-imposed obsta-cles and unnecessary blocks that have been created by our ego.

With this higher view of life, we see how petty people are, and how our minds can keep us imprisoned. We see how holding on to the past allows no room for the future to flourish. Mostly, we see how fear is the real culprit. When we banish the fear that pollutes our minds, we see how easily and readily available love is to solve all of life's problems. In addition, we comprehend the invaluable lessons with which un-happy situations provide us. We clearly see the choices that would be better for our souls' growth and the joy they would bring others. In the end, we become profoundly aware of our connectedness to every-one, how our thoughts have ripples that affect others in positive and negative ways.

I FOUND GOD

The following reading was done at my home. A friend of mine who was a priest had been very unhappy with himself and was seriously thinking about leaving the priesthood. At first, I was a little unsure that the messages that would come through would be what he wanted to hear. But as I always do, I asked for guidance from my spirit guides, said a prayer, and left the rest to God.

"Father Warren, are you comfortable?" I asked the priest.

"Ready, James."

I closed my eyes and suddenly felt a strong presence in the room. It was the figure of a nun.

"Warren, there is a nun standing here. She has an immense heart filled with love. It's quite powerful."

"I can feel her myself," Warren replied.

"She tells me that she loves you."

"Yes, I know. I love her too."

"Who's Margaret?" I asked.

"Sister Mary Margaret. That's her."

"*Follow your heart*, she is saying."

Suddenly, another spirit took shape. He was a small, stocky man dressed in priestly robes.

"There is someone else here now, Warren. He looks like a priest although he is wearing more colorful vestments."

"That must be Monsignor Egan."

"He is telling me that he didn't understand things when he first passed over."

"I don't understand," said Father Warren. "He was very devout. I am sure he went straight to heaven."

"He says that nothing was as he expected. There were no saints to greet him, no heaven like the one he was looking forward to. He expected an angelic choir and Jesus, but none of that happened."

Father Warren looked at me as if a bolt from out of the blue had hit him. "What does he mean?"

"He is saying that he never got anything that the church told him he would. The truth is that he wound up in the exact same place he would go to in prayer and contemplation. He is not in the heaven he used to believe in."

"That can't be," said Father Warren. "We're priests. We serve Jesus and the church. That's what I teach people. How is it that heaven doesn't exist?"

I looked at the priest with sympathetic eyes. "Monsignor *is* in heaven, but it's not a definitive place like you think." Looking upward, I added. "It's not up there. Heaven is where he is. God is not outside him. God is within him."

"I'm not sure I believe you, James."

I took a moment to clarify my thoughts with the monsignor.

"Monsignor is saying that, like Jesus, who ascended into heaven, we ascend only when we go within and discover our true self."

Father Warren quietly sat there listening.

"He wants you to know that you are a good priest. You have opened many people's hearts and started them thinking about the truth of their own souls. Don't be discouraged. He knows you are a rebel, but the church needs rebels to help it change and move forward."

It seemed that the reading was a real eye-opener for Father Warren. He called me several weeks later and said that he had decided to stay in the priesthood.

"You know, James, at first I was skeptical about what you said. Then I sat in prayer for a very long time. I could hear Monsignor Egan talking to me. I realized that everything I had said and done I did because it was taught to me in a certain way. I wasn't happy following the rules and following a certain pattern. Now I feel free to be who I am and to march to my own drummer, even if it's not exactly the way I was taught by the church. Things have to be updated, and I am going to teach people to trust in themselves and listen to God inside their hearts."

As Father Warren learned, the idea of seeing God clearly involves an inward seeing every bit as much as, if not more than, an outward one. Because we pay so much attention to the illusions of this physical world, we hold ourselves back from freedom by our attachments. We want to be free, but the illusion has become our reality, and it is so powerful. It becomes a never-ending cycle. We have to step out of the illusion and see the world from our hearts.

Thousands of spirits who have passed over have communicated to me that their departure was a gift to their loved ones left behind on earth. Their loved ones' grief and sorrow started many of them on an inner spiritual journey. Without experiencing the death of a loved one, their family members might not have looked beyond their physical shells. They would have stayed stuck in the world of illusion, never questioning what lies beyond. The presence of their dearly departed loved ones around them has given the living the impetus to seek beyond the physical world to a place within that satisfies their souls.

Mindful or Mindless?

When we start the journey of becoming aware of self and environment, we begin to live a *mind-full* life. Mindfulness is a way of looking at the larger world and our own particular life with the awareness of the present moment.

As you look at your daily life, you will probably see many examples of an absence of mindfulness. For instance, when you get a credit card bill, and it is much higher than you thought it would be, you might react: "What was I thinking?" Perhaps you're in a relationship that you know in your heart is not based on truth. You are merely filling some kind of void. Once again, you might ask: "What am I thinking?" The answer is clear. You were and are *not* thinking. If you are not aware of what you think, feel, and sense, you become a victim. You become the creator of situations that are to your own detriment.

In that recent demonstration in Reno, a man's spirit came through all rough and tough. He had died in a motorcycle accident. He did admit that he made a big mistake. He was not *mindful* enough to wear a helmet before he zoomed off down the road. His mindlessness cost him his life. It's easy to be mindless: losing glasses, misplacing keys, leaving the coffeepot on, forgetting someone's anniversary or birthday, not being sensitive to other people's feelings, and so forth.

When we live life with a lack of awareness, the mind and body go on autopilot. We react to people and situations based on old habits of perceiving, feeling, and behaving. When we live life as a routine, we deal with situations based on past hurts and betrayals. Without thinking, we respond as if those same old experiences were happening again. We go through life thinking about something else instead of living in the present moment. Therefore, life happens *to* us. We are no longer in charge of what happens. When we practice mindfulness we are constantly *re-minding* ourselves to see through new eyes.

Lack of awareness can have serious consequences. It certainly did for the man who didn't wear his helmet. By ignoring inner messages you can miss out on important moments in your life, especially ones affecting your relationships, health, and success. For instance, if your body is trying to give you a message about a health concern and you are busying your mind with trivialities or you are on autopilot, you won't sense the warning signals, and you may end up with a serious health crisis.

Just recently, I was with an old friend at dinner. I said to her, "I have often wondered why I live by the beach." I never really liked the beach per se, nor am I a sun worshiper. I do love surfing, though. Now when I say surfing, I do not mean I surf myself. I do, however, love to watch surfers as they ride the waves. I can spend hours watching them maneuver their boards above and through the formidable ocean. It becomes very meditative. For me, surfing is an analogy for life. Life is really a series of balancing acts. When we are mindful, we can center ourselves on the board, so that when problems arise (like a big wave), we can ride with calmness, joyfulness, and love right to the shore. Without mindfulness, we let our old, habitual behaviors and emotions cause us to wipe out in the tumultuous surf.

By managing our thoughts, we are less likely to be judgmental. Without thinking, it's too easy to fall into past responses when we are wronged. We end up saying things like, "That moron!" or "How stupid can they be?" or using even stronger, more hateful language. If we are mindful, we are aware of what comes out of our mouth. As we see things with clarity of consciousness, we can evaluate situations without falling back on past impulses and habits of thinking.

Mindfulness brings us into higher states of consciousness that give us unlimited freedom. When we are attuned to the higher levels of being, the lower levels of our nature and things previously hidden are illuminated. As we recognize the higher aspects of ourselves, we naturally become more intuitive, creative, and aware of people's feelings with a very different perspective. It is as if we are seeing them from a soul level and not merely the physical level. Doors are opened that were once closed to us.

IN PLAIN SIGHT

I looked at the last person to enter the beautiful St. Peter's Cathedral, where at least five hundred people were in attendance. She was dressed in a stylish suit, but seemed to be somewhat harried. As she quietly slipped into the back row, where she sat all by herself, she emitted a long sigh of relief. I began the demonstration with a prayer, and the room immediately became silent. Then I spoke about the spirit world and the number of spirits who had gathered all around the beautiful cathedral.

I began, "A spirit came to me last night, and I see him here again today. He is a slight man, with dark hair, wearing a light-colored jacket. He has a red book in his hand. He wants to contact his daughter." The woman in the very last row shot her left arm up in the air.

"Does this mean something to you, please?" I asked.

She nodded as I walked to the very back of the cathedral.

"Your dad mentions a red book. Do you know what this means?"

"Well, I had a dream about my father last night, and he was handing me a red book."

"Thank you. Your father wants to tell you that he is very proud of you. He says that you had to overcome many difficulties in your life, and he is very proud that you still want to be a healer. Do you understand?"

"Yes," the woman replied. "I am trying to decide whether I should drop my corporate career and devote my life to doing healing work and teaching. That's why I'm here. I've heard about your work, and I thought I might see if there was something here for me."

"What is your name, please?" I asked the woman.

"Chelsea."

"Your father is proud of you and wants to assist you."

Chelsea's face softened. Whatever fear she might have had seemed to have vanished.

"He is saying that you are right to do the work you want to do. He is also saying that you will be writing many books."

"Really?!" Chelsea said in astonishment.

"Your father is watching over you and your brothers."

"I'm glad. My brother is having a hard time."

"Is your father Asian?"

"Yes, he is from South Korea."

"He loves you very much. This is his message for you, your mother, and your two brothers. He also loves your half sister and half brother."

"I don't have a half sister or a half brother," Chelsea said.

"Well, ask your mother. He is saying that she has the story." I turned to Chelsea. "Sometimes, we don't know everything."

"I would know something like that," Chelsea insisted.

"Well, that is what he is telling me." I paused to hear the rest. "He is saying that this evening will change your life. You will begin to see yourself from a different perspective and a higher consciousness," I assured her.

Chelsea left the cathedral with many questions yet to be answered.

Several years after that event, I received a letter from a person named Shanté. She had changed her name from Chelsea, and she had written to describe her experience after her reading:

Dear James,

The day I went to your talk, I woke up early and felt tired from not getting enough sleep. I went into the kitchen and saw my mom sitting in the chair. Out of the blue she started to tell me that my dad sent a book to me about ten years ago. It was strange that she was even talking about him, because she doesn't talk about my dad. So I asked her to give me the book. That was the day I went to your talk.

When I returned home, I told my family about your reading, and they experienced a lot of healing. One other thing. You spoke about my half sister and brother, whom I never met or heard of. I asked my mom about them. She told me that we did indeed have a half sister and brother in Korea. Two months later, my brother went to Korea and found them. And, just a few days ago, my sister sent me pictures of her and my half brother's kids. I found myself crying while looking at the pictures, because they looked so much like my brothers and me. I still haven't met them, but we all feel such a strong bond between us now. I want to thank you, James, for this gift of confirmation that I am on a right path and that we are infinitely connected to everything, especially to the world beyond the physical world. I am in the process of writing my first book.

Shanté
Group Retreat Coordinator
Sedona Retreat Center

Since Shanté's letter to me, I have communicated with her and found out that she had been working as a corporate executive for a computer company and was very unhappy there. She told me that she was so moved by the whole situation with her father, half sister and brother, and my reading, that she began intense meditation to expand her consciousness. Once she did, her old way of life meant nothing to her. She quit her job and moved to Sedona to study. Presently, Shanté is a healing teacher assisting others to find their own paths.

Living life with clarity makes it easier for us to see that we are part of a multidimensional system. Time limits the physical world, but we as spiritual beings reside in timelessness. If in this state of higher consciousness we realize that we are not imprisoned by the limitations of the three-dimensional world, we will live life with new awareness. We will realize that there is a heavenly part of ourselves that we can access at any time in our daily lives. Consciousness cannot be lost, hurt, or fail because it is all-knowing. It is the light that illuminates ignorance and darkness. Our everyday problems and troubles can be understood from a new perspective, and the solutions will be easy to come by. Consciousness is our hope, our faith, and our love. It is all that we are and all that we will be. Once we arrive at this realization, we are no longer slaves of the three-dimensional world and are open to experiencing and receiving new levels of awareness and knowingness. This is the beginning of our transcendence.

PART FOUR

your new
LIFE

TEN

Transcendence

Teach this triple truth to all: A generous heart,
kind speech, and a life of service and compassion are
the things which renew humanity.

—Gautama Buddha

L ife is a magical journey, and one that, in the grand scheme of the cosmos, is over in the blink of an eye. When people exit the body at the time of death, their spirits experience an overwhelming sense of freedom, peace, and joy. There is an immediate impression that they are connected to the oneness of all things, that they are an integral piece of the cosmic puzzle. When souls first arrive on a higher plane of existence, their mental ability becomes overwhelmingly acute, and they are promptly and utterly aware of the thoughts, feelings, and words of loved ones left behind. Spirits realize that they were always spirits, but while on earth had physical experiences. Spirits don't suffer like we do. There is no more pain. Obstacles gradually melt away the more fully spirits enter into the light. Their perspective completely changes in every respect. We can benefit from their insightful words and messages without necessarily having to die first in order to experience a new transcendent state.

Near-Death Experience

The closest humans come to death without dying is in a near-death experience (NDE). Those who have had an NDE return from the brink of death with a unique perspective, and their lives seem to be forever changed because of it.

In my recent book *Ghosts Among Us,* I shared how my life changed after going through my own NDE. This time I want to share an NDE told to me by my close friend Erik. He lost control of his car while driving by a construction area of the freeway. As you will see, his experience is typical of someone who has had a profound, life-changing event:

> Immediately after hitting the steel girders, I felt myself floating out of my body and hovering above it. I was aware of all the people watching me, as I lay there paralyzed by the shock of what had just occurred. I remember looking down at my body and seeing it for the first time in a three-dimensional way. At first it was strange, but I knew I was still connected to it in some way. I have read somewhere that many times people don't relate to their bodies when they go through a near-death experience, but I did. I remember there was no pain whatsoever. I felt free, happy, and whole, and I knew that this was the real me. I was a happy and whole individual.
>
> As I looked down at my bloody and lifeless body, an enormous wave of compassion instantly washed over me, and I wanted to let everyone know I would be fine. I think everybody thought I was dead. They needed to know that this was only a temporary condition, but they could not hear my thoughts.

Then suddenly I felt myself being pulled at an enormous speed. I felt as if I was rising higher and higher, and I immediately became aware of a brilliant light. This light seemed all-knowing, yet it reminded me that I also had all this knowledge. Instinctively, I knew that everything I ever needed to know was already inside of me. I remember being aware that I was one with *all* the people on the planet simultaneously in that one moment. I realized that we were all connected. How can I explain it? I was aware of people in different countries involved in many types of activity at the same time. Overall, I knew that everyone was me, but in a different body. I was filled with a sense of depression from people in hospitals and prisons. I could see people praying in churches, mosques, and temples. I felt their intentions for the world and each other, even though they were not aware of each other's common thoughts and prayers.

As my awareness peaked, I was very conscious of the beautiful planet earth I called home. It was so extraordinary. I was aware of it breathing and pulsating much like a human body. It wasn't a big ball of lifeless matter, but very much alive. It shone like a shimmering blue and green jewel floating in the universe. As I looked closer, I could see some of the horrible destruction done to Mother Earth. It was like seeing inside a person's body that had tumors and blocked arteries. I could see a blackness of impending death. The earth was gasping for breath from the weight of pollution piercing into her body. I knew then that she was dying and needed help from me. I had to do something even though at the time I felt helpless.

At that instant, I remember thinking, "I can't go yet. My work is not done. I have to go back and save earth. I must tell others that this planet lives, and that we have a responsibility to keep her alive. We can't kill her!" But how could I go back and fix her when probably every bone in my body was broken?

A being of the light quickly filled me with the impression that
I was part of a divine plan, as is every person, and that my ultimate
purpose is to love and serve all sentient beings. I could tell that the
light-being understood all my fears and doubts. I was assured that
I would heal and be able to do the work necessary to feed my soul
and help Mother Earth.

The moment I had this thought, I was immediately back in my
body. I awakened to find myself lying on a gurney in an ambulance.
I could hear the sound of the siren as two paramedics knelt over
me, both faces filled with apprehension and concern. I smiled and
heard one of them say, "We got him back." Yes, you could say I
came back that day. I came back in a new light and with a new
perspective. I have since been involved in many green projects and
have created organizations all over the world to save the planet.
Since my experience, I have never looked at life, death, and people
the same. I honor everyone I come in contact with, especially myself.

The experiences of people like my friend have been documented in
numerous books on the subject of near-death experiences. If this is
truly a glimpse into multidimensional reality, then we cannot ignore
the message that all of these experiences share. We are all one on a living planet, and only our egos, fears, and beliefs separate us.

We do not need to have a near-death experience, however, to change
our perspective about life. As we walk upon this earth, involved with
situations and problems that seem so overwhelming, we should view
problems as stepping-stones on our way to freeing our minds. Every
time we are given a challenging experience, we need to recognize there
must be two sides to the story. If it is something negative and harsh, we
must try and see the positive side of it. Sometimes it feels like a scav-
enger hunt, as we try to uncover the joy and love that are part of the
difficult experience. And sometimes they may not reveal themselves so
easily, which means we must learn patience and faith by knowing in

our heart that there is a higher lesson at work. We just have to have the courage to discover the lesson hidden within the experience and learn it. Once we have gone through an experience and know the lesson that has been given to us, we will know what to expect in the future and, more importantly, we will be able to teach others how they can react in a similar circumstance.

Move Out of the Past

The mind is the most important determinant of our well-being and happiness. However, one of the most common hurdles the mind has to clear is living in the past. I know someone who is forever talking about her past and especially her childhood. She recalls every little situation with her mother and father while she was growing up. She recalls the jokes her daddy used to tell everyone, and how they would laugh. She talks about how she learned to dance at weddings with her uncles. Inevitably, when your mind is always in the past, you fall back into the mental and emotional state that you lived then. Perhaps my friend's inner child never got the attention she needed and is still looking for that love.

Unfortunately, like my friend, many adults relive their childhoods by holding on to certain behaviors and hurts that occurred way back when. How they felt about themselves at that time is how they feel now. When those childhood memories are jarred by hurts they experience as adults, they immediately regress to the reaction they had, unconsciously or consciously, as children. At this point, either they can refuse to confront the issue and let things stay as they are, or they can blame someone else for the situation, or they can finally take responsibility for what is happening and break the patterns of the past. If they choose the last option, they can finally let that inner child heal, grow up, and be an adult. When people make the appropriate changes within themselves to heal past wrongdoings, they are in a state of transcendence, and with that comes freedom to face any situation in life from an adult perspective.

The past has no power over us unless we give it that power. We no longer need to live in the past or even to blame our parents for every situation in our lives. It is up to us to take responsibility for the choices we make.

I have received so many letters from people who say they were abused while growing up, and because of their abuse, they can never have a normal emotional relationship. It is true that emotional traumas in childhood stay with us. When these traumas turn into a pattern of victimization, we are unable to find happiness in any area of life, not only in relationships, but also in jobs, finances, and friendships. People who are victims play a never-ending tape about how miserable life is, how nobody understands them, and how people take advantage of them. Releasing the past mind-set and replacing it with a positive outlook is the only way to come out of the shadows and into the light.

Your True Self

Another block to transcendence is staying in relationships that do not work. If we play a character to please other people instead of being who we are, we will never come into our own power or know the uniqueness of our own true being. I have found that most relationships are not based on honesty. People have agendas; they want something from us, such as financial security, a better station in life, acclamation, fame by association, or getting back at someone else. We must be willing to face the fact that some relationships are not for our highest good and can actually keep us from achieving our true potential. At first, this can be extremely difficult to admit to ourselves. No one ever likes to accept that a relationship may not be right for us and in fact should be ended. However, as we evolve, the world around us evolves as well. Those in our lives may not evolve at the same pace as we do and, in the end, we are the company we keep.

Our lack of self-esteem and self-trust constantly get in the way of our self-realization. If we do not believe in our own opinions, we are telling ourselves that we have *no power*. This lack of belief in ourselves causes us to make devastating, self-destructive decisions. When we can't determine who is worthy of our trust, we tend to bring people into our lives whom we find out much later we cannot trust at all. In order to be trusting we must discern and develop a sense of ourselves by listening to that little voice inside our heads. That little voice is our intuition. People often confuse intuition with fear. If the answer you hear inside of you is one of fear, that is not your intuition. Intuition is your sixth sense and the best measure of understanding the world around you. Intuition is usually a gut feeling; it is not logical thinking. When you don't listen to your gut feelings, you usually end up making mistakes. You must learn to effectively utilize this God-given tool and let it be productive in your life. Using your intuition is part of learning to transcend your lower self.

Finally, the strongest obstacle to transcendence, and the one that I have mentioned often enough in this book, is *fear*. As previously stated, fear can freeze us in place and stop us from growing. It completely takes away our power, our sense of self, and an effective view of the world around us. Fear is the reason we live so much in the past. It constantly reminds us that there are things that still need *fixing*. Fear also justifies bad behavior, leaving us to make excuses about why we do the things we do. For instance, religious extremists use fear to manipulate others. They take away people's decision-making power by feeding them fear-based doctrine. It is so unfortunate that so many people use fear to control others, but if we did not believe in fear in the first place, no one could control anyone.

MY MIND IS FREE

When I do my demonstrations, I usually start by explaining how I got involved in this work and then go on to clarify the process of communication. I do this for many reasons. People come to the event from many different backgrounds and with different belief systems and expectations. Some are nervous, others curious, and still others are unsure and skeptical. My introduction is not just a formality, but an attempt to establish rapport with the audience and help them feel at ease. I am showing them that I am a normal, everyday guy, and there is nothing weird, strange, or *otherworldly* about me. I usually crack some jokes and, with any luck, people laugh. Once they recognize that I am like them, they begin to let down their guard.

As I explain about spirit phenomena, I clairvoyantly scan the audience and usually see some very interesting sights. I definitely see the auras of everyone in the audience. Auras look like envelopes shaped around physical bodies. Some people have smooth, expansive auras in lovely pastel colors, while others have dark, clouded envelopes with holes and tears. Some of these tears and holes can be caused by extreme emotional trauma or addictions like drugs and alcohol.

In order for me to get the optimum energy to work with spirits, I need to raise the energy of the entire group to make it more receptive. This is accomplished by helping participants to be in an open, healing, and receptive place. How do I do this? Inevitably there are rows of spirit guides, many dressed in various colored robes, in the audience. These guides are there to pull dark and heavy energy out of a person's aura. Heavy energy is caused by mental depression, worry, emotional pain, and from other people's negative thoughts attached to the aura. Sometimes guides will comment on how difficult it is to get through to individuals because their auras are blocked with fear, depression, unhappiness, and lack of self-love. It would be like trying to clean bugs off our windshields after traveling on a long road trip.

Additionally, during my workshops I begin with a guided medita-tion to assist in clearing people's energy and the energy of the space in order to get better reception. It would be akin to cleaning off the ter-minals of a car battery. To connect with spirits and be able to be influ-enced by the higher forces of love and creativity, we must keep ourselves in good running order.

The following reading is a wonderful example of how a woman let obstacles block her from living life to the fullest. It happened during one of my demonstrations in Los Angeles. It always amazes me when I walk into a room filled with hundreds or thousands of people and see spirits line up behind me and around individuals in the audience. Usu-ally, most people are eager to hear from their loved ones. However, there are always exceptions. Some people are dragged to demonstra-tions literally kicking and screaming, because they refuse to open themselves up to something new. One such woman was in the audience that night. Her friends brought her "against her better judgment."

A female spirit stood beside this woman. I hesitated for a moment before walking over to her side of the ballroom.

"May I speak to you, please?" I asked.

She stared at me as if to say, "Go away."

I stood there watching the spirit next to her. She seemed determined to get her message across. So I continued in spite of my icy reception.

"Who's Doris?" I asked.

The woman's head shot straight up. "That's me."

"Doris, there is a woman standing next to you. She seems anxious for you to hear her."

"I can't imagine who that might be."

"I am getting a big G, Gina, Georgy, something like that. Does that name mean anything to you?"

"I grew up with a Georgia. She was one of my childhood friends, but we drifted apart when I moved to California. I knew she died, but . . ."

"Well, she's here with you now."

"I really can't believe it. We hardly spoke the last few years of her life."

"Time doesn't mean anything to those who pass. She is telling me that she has been watching out for you. She knows that you are not receptive to things like this. She wants you to know that you can change your life even now."

"Change from what?" Doris snapped.

"Georgia is saying that you had a pretty bad childhood. That is why you are so closed down. You live a lot in your past. You feel sorry for yourself a lot."

The more I spoke, the more Doris froze up. I could see swirls of dark gray around her head and chest.

"Georgia says that she understands now. She was a lot like you. She didn't believe in an afterlife until she died. She knows now that she could have been happier. She sees how her negative thinking shut out the good stuff."

Doris didn't budge.

"Georgia says that she will try to help you. She whispers to you a lot, but you just ignore what she is trying to tell you. She says that the things you were brought up to believe are not true. She wants you to not be so depressed and to do more things that make you happy. Do you understand?"

"Frankly, I don't know what you are talking about. My life is just fine. Can you please go on to someone else?"

Doris's comment shocked me.

Then suddenly a spirit couple showed up. I could tell these were Doris's parents.

"Your parents are here, Doris. They want to tell you that they love you. Your mother especially wants to say that she is sorry."

I could see Doris's eyes fill with tears.

"They want you to be happy. They didn't know about life, and they taught you what they were taught. They were fearful about so many things. *Don't be afraid,* they are saying."

"I just can't believe you. My parents were alcoholics. They made my life miserable. How can they be happy now when they were so unhappy when they were alive?"

The audience sat quietly. Apparently, Doris's comment struck a nerve for many.

"They are saying they are sorry. They didn't know any better. They had a lot to learn, and they are still learning. They don't want you to follow in their footsteps. Are you familiar with a black-and-white photo of a little girl wearing a jumper sitting on a tricycle?"

Doris's eyes opened wide. "That's a picture of me when I was seven. How could you know that?"

"Your mother is pointing to the photo. It's on top of a red desk."

Doris nodded her validation.

"Thank you," I said, my frustration easing. "Now do you believe me?"

"I suppose so."

"Your father is jumping in now. He is saying that he enjoys life now. He feels so free. He says that he wishes he could hug you and tell you how much he loves you. He wishes he could have felt the freedom in life that he now feels. He says, *Don't worry so much. Life is worth living.*"

On that note, feeling exhausted from the reading, I turned to the audience and said, "Let's take a break."

You may think that this is the end of the story, but it's not. Several years after this particular reading with Doris, I was in Minneapolis on a lecture tour. There must have been at least a thousand people in attendance at one lecture. Midway through my readings, I saw a female spirit beside a woman. She was waving her hand like crazy. I had to go find out what she wanted to say.

It's me. It's me, the spirit called out.

I stood by an elderly woman with white hair. "There is a woman next to you waving her hand." Suddenly I realized that I knew this spirit woman. I was sure I had seen her before.

It's me, Doris. Remember me?

"Do you know someone named Doris?" I asked.

The white-haired woman shook her head.

"She is an old friend from high school. She is showing me a picture of a yearbook."

"Oh my God," said the woman. "Could it be Doris Franklin? We worked on the senior yearbook together."

James, it's me Doris, the spirit said. *Doris——the woman who didn't believe you. You spoke to me.*

Suddenly I remembered the woman from years back who was so closed off. I couldn't believe that it was the same Doris. She seemed so vibrant and cheerful.

"I know this woman," I said. "I did a reading for her a few years ago when she was alive. She was sitting in the audience just like you folks."

There was a gasp.

"She wants to say she is sorry for not believing." I turned to the audience to explain. "She was so stubborn and could not accept the message from a spirit. Now she knows for herself that it was the truth."

Then I looked at Doris's friend. "She wants you to be happy. She sees that her negative thinking made her miserable and her body sick. She is saying that she used to drink a lot. She is showing me her body filled with dark masses. She died of cancer."

"Really?" Doris's friend uttered.

"Doris is telling me that she was so skeptical of me and what I had told her. Now she is saying, *Believe!*"

"It's funny you should say that. I was afraid to come here. I'm Catholic. It's not right for Catholics to come to things like this."

I smiled. "I was Catholic once myself."

I continued with Doris's thoughts. "Your friend Doris wants you to know that what they teach you is not entirely true. She says she found herself in sort of a dark place when she passed over. It took friends and family to convince her that life can be what you make it.

She had to be healed of a lot of pain. She is saying, *You have to think of what you want and let God give it to you.*"

The white-haired woman seemed surprised. "Gee, that isn't the Doris I knew. She always seemed so down."

"Well, that's what she wants you to understand. Don't be down on yourself. You are more than what you think you are. She says that when you pass, she'll be there to greet you. Meanwhile, she is saying that you have many years left to do what you really want to do. *Do it!* she says."

"I'll try. Thanks, Doris."

I love spirit messages from those I have met before they pass over. As with Doris, I usually see a change when they come back as spirits. It rarely happens, but when it does, it motivates me even more to teach others about the illusionary prisons in which we place our minds. It's up to *you* to change your life and move on to a new way of experiencing the world around you.

The Golden Rule

In order to strive for greater perfection and joy in our lives and reach spiritual transcendence, we must be conscious of others. We must step out of self-centeredness and be sensitive and mindful every day that we are part of everyone else. By now, you have read many examples in which spirits show that we are all *one*. For me, being aware of this knowledge and using it every day have accelerated my self-realization. Once I take the focus away from myself, I become cognizant of my own capacity to give to, sympathize with, and love another.

One of my favorite movies of all time is *To Kill a Mockingbird*, based on the Pulitzer Prize–winning novel by Harper Lee. At the end of the movie, the daughter, Scout, says something profound, something her father, Atticus Finch, once taught her as a child. The words obviously lodged an indelible place in her soul and in my mind: "You never truly know someone until you've stood in their shoes and walked around in them."

These words are the essence of the Golden Rule: "Do unto others as you would have others do unto you." This universal rule seems so obvious that it's impossible for anyone not to grasp it. I know how I would like to be treated, so how hard can it be for me to treat others the same way? I am sure most of us have heard a reprimanding parent say to a child, "Is that how you want to be treated?" The Golden Rule is part of many speeches, sermons, and even many a defense lawyer's summation. The message is a fundamental component of most world religions.

However, to spout the Golden Rule is one thing, but to live it is another. When I began to incorporate this way of thinking into my daily life, I found that it wasn't enough for me just to do good acts and treat people decently. I had to understand why a person behaved in a certain way; I had to comprehend the motives behind another person's actions. To paraphrase Atticus Finch, I had to stand in another person's shoes and look at the world from that point of view. Whether people were homeless, closed-minded, politically motivated, or extremely wealthy, I had to slip into their skin and attempt to see life from their eyes.

To say the least, it was an educational endeavor. It taught me how to be sympathetic toward others. I realized that people act in response to their own cultural, economic, and educational backgrounds. It definitely taught me how to have compassion for people as well as strengthened my desire to alleviate the suffering they were going through.

During the desegregation of the 1960s, John F. Kennedy asked white Americans to imagine being looked down upon and treated badly based on the color of their skin. He challenged them to treat others as if they were the same as themselves. Recently, California citizens were asked to vote on Proposition 8, an amendment to the state's constitution that would deny gay people the right to marry. Those opposed to denying rights to gays ran ads on television asking people to imagine how they would feel if they were not allowed to marry someone they loved. Again, much of the dispute over the right of gay people to marry came from religious groups that pandered to people's fears. If these folks walked in a gay person's shoes, perhaps they would see that what gays want, as far as happiness is concerned, is the same as what straight people want. Judgment and ridicule would soon disappear.

As I write this book, the biopic of Harvey Milk entitled *Milk* is in theaters. Harvey Milk was the nation's first openly gay man to be elected to political office as a city supervisor in San Francisco. Dan White, another city supervisor, assassinated him and Mayor George Moscone in 1978. The movie stayed with me for days. I found the sadness of Milk's untimely death and the subsequent ruling on his murder very disturbing. Dan White was given a mere five years in prison for two murders. It seemed like a mild punishment for taking the lives of two people. I decided to dig into the facts a little more. I wanted to understand the mind of a person who would resort to such a crime. I looked into the background of Dan White, and the more I delved into his history, the more I grasped where he was coming from. I would never condone this man's actions, but for him to believe that murder was his only option is incredibly sad.

When I meditated on this incident, I realized a few things about Dan White. He struggled not only with mental illness, but also with his Catholic religion, his own sexuality, and expectations imposed on him by others. Taking a human life is wrong. But as much as we want to loathe this type of person, we must try and understand the motivation behind such an act. What are the person's background and beliefs? When I studied Dan White, I realized that he was taught to use a gun by our own government during his service in Vietnam. It seemed paradoxical to give a gun to someone who was unstable, perhaps one step away from committing murder, in the name of preserving and protecting our political and economic interests. It was too bad.

Many spirits have told me that the Golden Rule is the doorway to human understanding. They have said that if they could have seen others as themselves, their lives would have been less of a struggle, and they would have generated more love than hate.

THE GIFT OF FORGIVENESS

This next reading was very sad. It took place in Chicago many years ago. After my introduction and meditation, I began scanning the room, as I have done so many times before. There was a male spirit in the back of the room. He was a thin, wiry, curly-haired young man. I was drawn to this spirit.

"There is a young man in this area who seems somewhat disturbed. He has dark curly hair. Does this mean anything to anyone?"

No one moved. I knew that I had to get more information from the spirit. I stood in the midst of the audience communicating with the dead man.

"He says he was murdered. He has come back to forgive his murderer."

The audience exclaimed their shock.

Suddenly I was drawn to a small, plump woman with short, blonde hair. "Was your son murdered?" I asked her.

"No. My son is in prison."

The audience reacted once again.

"This young man standing next to you says he forgives you."

The woman shook her head in confusion.

I listened for more facts. "Is your son in prison for murder?"

The short-haired woman's head bowed in affirmation.

"This young man is the person your son killed!" I said with astonishment.

Yet another cry of surprise emerged from the audience.

"I am so sorry," the woman blurted out. "My son didn't mean it. I'm sure he didn't."

"Who is Alfred or Alfonse?"

"Alfonso Melia," the woman added. "He is the person my son murdered."

"Alfonso is saying he forgives your son."

The woman began to weep. "Please tell Alfonso that I am so sorry. I didn't teach my son to be so hateful. I am so ashamed."

"Alfonso is showing me his death. He was beaten by your son. Is this right?"

"Yes."

"Alfonso says he visits your son on death row. He tries to help him."

"My son was very disturbed. He hung out with the wrong crowd. He became very prejudiced against certain people."

"Was your son part of a gang? I see him with a group of young men with tattoos."

"Yes. I didn't know it until it was too late. These kids hated Mexicans, Jews, and gays. Donny, my son, was brainwashed by these kids. He was such a good boy when he was young."

"Alfonso is saying that he was picked on because he spoke with an accent. He says that he was in the wrong place at the wrong time." I felt so sorry for the woman. "Alfonso understands that your son was under a lot of pressure from his friends. He forgives him for not knowing any better."

The woman seemed so flustered.

I turned to the audience. "Here is a young man who was killed because he looked different from others. How troubled are we as humans to want to kill someone because he looks different, acts differently, or speaks differently than the rest of us? This young man is here to teach us the value of treating others as we would want to be treated. This is valuable advice, because what we believe here on earth we will take with us. It's a lesson for all of us to learn."

I turned to the woman. "This young man forgives you. It's your turn to forgive yourself and your son. It will help you both to heal."

So many of us are taught to hate rather than love. We are taught to be prejudiced. We are taught to attack others who are different from us. We are taught that if we don't take something, someone else will take it. We are not born with these ideas. These ideas are instilled in us as children. It is difficult to reverse these impressions, but it's not impossible. As the Stephen Sondheim lyric goes, "Careful the things you say, children will listen . . ."

We have to relearn, and there are many ways to do just that. We have to become as little children, but this time we must be our own teachers, so that we can live our lives anew with support and love.

ELEVEN

Living Your Life

*And in the end, it's not the years in your life that
count. It's the life in your years.*

—Abraham Lincoln

I f limitations are imposed on us from a very young age, how can we possibly live freely? Life is a series of ironies. We are limitless souls, but we live in a world of limitations. We were taught to look at and be in this world based on this limited viewpoint. We are not naturally materialistic beings, but because we are in a materialistic, three-dimensional world, we have acquired a materialistic consciousness. We accept that this world is *real* without question, and yet in truth this world is merely a transient place for our souls to enter in order to gain greater understanding and to decipher the many facets of love.

Because we are soul beings, we are individually equipped with incredible inner resources. Our soul nature allows us to manifest anything we desire as long as we put our minds and hearts into what we want. However, there is a catch. Because we live in a limited three-dimensional, physical world, we feel somewhat separated from our spiritual essence and have forgotten that we are actually spiritual beings with limitless power.

Many spirits often speak to me of their disappointments during their brief walk on earth. They wish they had spent more time focusing on their inner selves rather than busying their outer selves with tasks. They wish they had taken that extra five minutes to listen to someone's troubles, even if they didn't know how to help. They wish they had slowed down enough on their way out their door or garage to wave hello or give a kind word to a neighbor. Mostly they feel as though they wasted so much valuable time focusing on physical, material goals instead of expressing love in some small way. They realize how their thoughts affected not only their lives, but also the lives of all those with whom they came in contact. Often when they look back at what they have left behind, they wonder if they could have left the world a little bit better place than when they arrived.

Many souls recognize how foolish they have been and how unaware they were of their spiritual power. They feel they had unwittingly given their power away to family, friends, and even society. They were so locked into a limited mind-set, they could not see the miracles waiting outside their doors. They have said to me that even though their humanness was limited, their spiritual selves were endless. Because they were stuck, they didn't take hold of life and create something out of it. They were victims of their own wrong thinking and clouded perception and were denied joyful living. In their own way, spirits have said that we need to stand up and realize that everything we need for a positive, blissful life is already inside us. The spirit world insists that we must recognize the divine aspect of our beings. So if we want to live a new life, we must discover our divinity. Prayer, meditation, therapy, and yoga are but a few roads that lead to a relationship with our divine selves.

Believe in Yourself

There is no one that knows you better than yourself. Yes, it's true that we have been taught to look to others for our answers, but only you know what works for you and what doesn't. Therefore, you should never let others' opinions define who you are. They don't know you well enough. This doesn't mean that what other people have to say is not valuable, but you must realize that it is purely their opinion and not necessarily true for you. Over time, you will go through many trials and tribulations in order to have a better appreciation of and trust in yourself. But in order to reach this awareness, you must be willing to withstand the critical opinions and beliefs of others and see those opinions and beliefs for what they are—merely someone else's point of view.

I can't tell you how many times an ignorant critic has made a sweeping statement about me and my work without ever meeting me or knowing anything about the basics of mediumship. As a pioneer in this spiritual movement, I knew that many a harsh word and inappropriate act would come my way, and many times my character and integrity would be called into question. That was just part of the territory. Anytime someone asks people to change their belief systems about life and death in order to lift the veil of ignorance and narrow-mindedness, there will always be judgment and criticism by others with a different point of view and a different belief system.

You may ask why I would let others get away with their criticism of me. Don't I have any self-respect? Well, of course I do. But it's not about me, the messenger; it's about the message. I must look at the bigger picture. My job is to help people open their minds to new ideas about life and death. When I began my work, I knew deep inside me that this was my soul's calling. I knew that if I followed my heart and did the work, many people would be healed.

It doesn't matter what others think of you if you are fulfilling your life's purpose. If you worry about what other people think or say, you give away your power, and that is a surefire way to live an unfulfilled life. You must not try to be like others. Be original. Speak differently, act differently, and work differently. A spiritless person lacks courage and energy. Remember the child you once were? Before you were called a hurtful name or told to shut up and stay out of sight, there was that wonderful child filled with imagination and wonder. You felt you could do and be anything. That child is the essence of who you are. That wonder is still there inside. It is your limitless spiritual power.

HIDING HER TRUTH

The following reading typifies a soul who lost her true self by trying to fit into someone else's idea of what she should be. I was in Denver as part of a weekend spirituality workshop. Toward the end of my readings, a spirit stood beside a young, attractive black woman.

I looked over to the woman sitting down and asked her, "Do you know the name Janet?"

The woman looked down, then raised her head and tentatively replied, "I had a great-aunt named Janet. But I didn't know her. She died before I was born."

"Do you know if she painted?"

"I have no idea."

"Who's Sarah?"

"That's my name."

"Well, Sarah, your aunt Janet knows who you are." I paused to listen to Janet. "She is showing me four children. Do you understand?" I asked Sarah.

"My grandmother had one brother and one sister."

"No. These are Janet's children. I guess they would be your second cousins."

"I have cousins in another state, but we really don't talk to each other."

"Your aunt is sounding sad to me. She says that she kept getting married and having children although she really didn't want to."

"I've heard my mother talk about Aunt Janet's husbands. I always thought Aunt Janet was a, well . . . flighty."

"That's not it," I quickly replied. "She says that she had to get married because that's what women in her time had to do. Women could not be single. It was not respectable. When one husband died, she had to find another. Having children was part of the package too."

"I didn't know that."

"She says that she liked to draw and paint, but was told that she had no talent and not to waste her time. Besides, she says, back then a black person was not thought of as artistic. She says that she is happy to be teaching art in the spirit world now. Her work hangs in galleries there."

"Really? That's fantastic! I have to ask my mother about all of this."

"Please ask your mother. Many times spirits come through, and we don't recognize them. But then when we get home and ask others about them, we find out that what they have said is true. Your great-aunt was sad most of her life. She says that she did what was expected and never did what she really wanted."

I turned to the audience. "We're lucky. A lot of the restrictions placed on people years ago about marriage, divorce, and children are not the same today, especially for women. All the more reason to express ourselves to the fullest. If we don't live our truth, it will come back to haunt us."

I turned back to Sarah. "Your aunt is saying that she was alone at the end of her life. Her husbands all died, and her children deserted her. She died penniless."

"That's sad. I really don't know much about her life."

"Your aunt says that you were sisters in another life. That's why she's here tonight. She says that you will share another life together in the future."

"This is unbelievable."

"Believe it. Ask your mother about your aunt. I would love to hear from you about this."

"I will. Thank you."

Several weeks later, I received an e-mail from Sarah. She said that she did speak with her mother, and what I had said was true:

When I told my mother about my aunt being artistic, she said that there was a box in the attic with Aunt Janet's stuff. So I took a look and found a beautiful painting by her. She seemed to be quite a talented artist, but I didn't really know. So, on a whim I took her painting to a gallery. I was shocked when they offered me $2,000 for the painting. I decided to keep it. Too bad she never saw the results of her work.

So I say to you, share your *own* perfect design with the rest of the world. That is how you will stand out. Let your light shine for all to see. Spirits often say that they didn't realize how fast life goes by. Life *is* fleeting. So make your mark on the time line of life. You can start by smiling and laughing more often. Enjoy yourself, and enjoy the ride. Don't take life so seriously. It's just a game.

Difficulties come and go. Money is made and lost. But *you* will never cease to be. You have control over your will and, therefore, your life. It doesn't matter what role you play, whether it is a servant or head of state; it is what you do with your role that matters. Don't try and play someone else's role; play your own. Do the most with what you are given. Knowing yourself is the source of change for your life. We change our reality by changing what is within us. This is our place of wholeness. The more we take responsibility for our reality, the quicker we will grow.

As you raise your consciousness and attune yourself to this inward power, you are able to release patterns of fear and trouble that have been in your earthly mind this lifetime and, perhaps, prior lifetimes. When you start to enter a period of becoming whole once again, you will be able to let go of obstacles like dishonesty, hatred, fear, and anger, which keep you from your truth. As you consistently practice aligning your intentions with divine light, your thoughts, words, and deeds will follow suit. In other words, you must be vigilant. You can't think positively one minute, then tell yourself that you are worthless the next. Consistent, persistent thoughts, words, and deeds are the key to change. Only then can you illuminate deep-rooted problems, perceive them for just what they are, and not let them define and defeat you. You will begin to experience life in a brand-new way. Your fears and negative emotions will no longer imprison you. You really will become the liberated whole being you always were, and you will feel free to live life to the highest expression of your being. As the saying goes: "The truth shall set you free."

MY HIGHER SELF

In order to live a life that is fulfilled and rich, one without regrets, you must discipline yourself to be mindful by seeing the world from a larger perspective. It is only when you can bring yourself into a relationship with your higher, divine power that you can begin to see your value in the world and to see in all the experiences of life, whether positive or negative, profound meaning. Your divine power is called by many names, among them Higher Self, Christ Consciousness, and Creative Source. Whether or not you are aware of it, you are guided by this creative spiritual power, for it is part of your soul's makeup. When you become conscious of this Higher Self, it is as if you have ascended a stairway and stepped out of a fog. You realize that you are something much greater than physical self.

The more you uncover the mysteries of the Universe, the more you will find that there is more to learn. The farther you go in your journey, the more you will realize how effortlessly the Universe provides what you need. Spiritual growth means that you are aware of the laws of the Universe and can regularly use them to bring unlimited love, health, and significant opportunities into your experience.

About twelve years ago I arranged for a group of thirty people to visit the spiritual centers of Brazil. Unbeknownst to me at the time, this would be the first of many expeditions to come. To me, Brazil is one of the most mystical places on earth, and the inhabitants are some of the warmest people I have ever met. I was blown away by their openness and candid awareness of their spiritual heritage. At this point in my life, I had been meditating and been on my own spiritual quest for a very long time. Through meditation, I had connected with my Higher Self. It is fairly easy to know when we are connected to our Higher Selves, because our thoughts and impressions are at a higher level. We see life from a loving viewpoint irrespective of its flaws and imperfections. And we know that our life's purpose is to contribute our talents and abilities to make the Universe whole and complete.

The weekly ceremony of one particular center in Brazil was similar to a shamanic journey or a Native American sweat lodge in that it lasted about six hours and was amazingly transformative. Participants interacted with the spirit world during the weekly ceremonies in a somewhat unorthodox way. To help them attune themselves to the higher frequencies of the spiritual dimensions, they drank Hiawatha tea. This tea, commonly known to many groups in South America, is considered sacred because of its hallucinogenic properties. The leaves are picked from a vine in the Amazon rain forest and have been used for centuries in this part of the world. Many indigenous tribes use some sort of substance in their spiritual quests to heighten awareness, eliminate the fears and phobias of the earthly mind, and communicate with the higher part of their beings.

My host, the priest of this intriguing congregation, explained to me upon our arrival, "We don't know what will happen. We may see the Virgin Mary or other entities. Each experience is unique and will be healing in one way or another."

The priest offered me the tea, and I drank a cup. Several minutes later, the ceremony began. I took my seat in a corner as an observer. The rest of the congregation began reciting ceremonial prayers. After fifteen minutes, I noticed my sense of perception beginning to alter dramatically. Voices became louder, then softer. The energy of the room became very, very intense. I had to remind myself to keep grounding myself, lest I become completely out of control. I was aware of many spirits in ceremonial dress around the room. As my eyes closed, I began to experience visions. These visions were different from any I have ever had before. There were such vivid, bright, glistening colors that it seemed as if I was staring at the center of a colossal diamond.

Then I felt as if I was transported to another place. I saw a person standing in front of me in a robe of purple and gold, wearing a gold turban. His intense, deep blue eyes transfixed me. As I observed him, I had a strong sense that I knew him and had always known him. He communicated with me telepathically and handed me a gold ring with a six-pointed amethyst in it. He told me that it was the spirit world's acknowledgment that I was an initiate. It seemed to be a great honor. I did not know exactly how to interpret this information, and I asked, "Who are you?" In the instant I asked the question, I knew the answer. I was staring at *myself*! Not the human James, but my Higher Self, the soul of James. This was probably one of the most profound experiences of my life.

A week later my group went to Salvador, Bahia, located in the northeastern part of Brazil. When we arrived, we shopped around for souvenirs. Marilyn, one of my guests, was at a jewelry store looking at various trays of stones. Quite impulsively, I asked the shopkeeper, "Do you carry any amethyst rings?"

She seemed a little taken aback. "Well, not usually. We only carry stones, as you can see. But a customer came in here many weeks ago and ordered an amethyst ring. We made it to his specifications, but he never came back."

The shopkeeper bent down and opened a drawer under the glass display case.

"Here it is." She held up the ring.

It was my turn to be taken aback. In front of me was the exact same gold and amethyst ring I had seen in my vision. I tried it on and, yes, it fit perfectly.

I looked at the shopkeeper. "You know, this ring really belongs to me."

Without hesitating, she replied, "Yes, I have been waiting for you to come and pick it up."

Marilyn stared first at me, then the ring. I patted her hand and said, "I think we are done here."

Meditations to Reconnect to Your Power

Through the years, people have asked me questions about how to live spiritually while struggling with the mundane matters of everyday life.

"How can I be aware of my Higher Self?"

"How can I know the reason for coming back to the earth at this time?"

"How can I become aware of my spirit guides and deceased loved ones who have passed?"

As you may have gathered by now, the initial step to finding answers to these questions is to reconnect with your divine nature. Just know there is a higher, more powerful part of *you*. Your Higher Self will come through to you in various ways: intuition, coincidences, and synchronicity of all kinds. As you strengthen your connection with your Higher Self by following through on your hunches as well as taking time to go within during meditation and prayer, your revelations and insights will increase. The following exercises will help you to attune to this power.

Meditation is much easier than people realize. You don't need to chant, repeat a mantra, or even count your breaths. Merely sit quietly and be aware of your thoughts. Many people tell me that they can't meditate, no matter how hard they try. My response is, "Don't *try*." When you meditate, do so without any expectations whatsoever. The only rule to follow with meditation is to do it on a regular basis, perhaps at the same time every day, so you get into a routine. After a while, it will become second nature to you.

Another important point to remember is that when you first start practicing, you will experience what is known as mind chatter, or extemporaneous and random thoughts like, "What time is it?" "How long do I have to sit here?" "What am I going to have for dinner?" Thoughts like these will inevitably pop into your head. Accept these thoughts and don't judge them by thinking, "I shouldn't be thinking this" or "This is not working." Instead, let these thoughts glide by you. Here's my analogy for meditation. Think of yourself floating down a river on a raft. Every once in a while a rock or wild rapid will get in the way, and you will have to float around the obstacle. Meditation is a lot like floating in your mind. You have to stay in the moment and float around your mundane thoughts. With regular practice, you will go into a deep place inside where your heart starts to open and speaks to you.

Heart-Self Meditation

Sit erect in a chair and close your eyes. Become aware of the pattern of each inhalation and exhalation of breath. Slowly begin to become mindful of each part of your body and acknowledge it. Start with your toes, feet, ankles, legs, and go on to your torso, back, chest, shoulders, arms, fingers, neck, and head. Next, concentrate on your heart area, or the center of love. Imagine a beautiful green and golden light of love emerging from your heart and flowing all through your body, from the top of your head, down the arms and legs and toes, and throughout your body. Don't stop the light at the fingertips, head, or toes. Let it float right out through these areas. Experience this loving energy for several seconds. Reflect on how it affects your body when you acknowledge its existence.

Next, imagine in your mind's eye that you are on a celestial elevator. With your loving, light-filled body, you step inside and begin to ascend higher and higher. Instead of floors, there are various levels of perception. As you ascend, your sense of self seems to expand. The floors are each represented by different bright colors, any colors you wish. When the elevator stops, you have arrived on the floor of Higher Knowing. The elevator opens, and there to greet you is your Higher Self. The first thing you might notice is the wisdom and love of your Higher Self. Get off the elevator and acknowledge your true self. You notice that you share all the same physical characteristics with your Higher Self. It is almost like looking at a twin, just more refined, untouched by physical matter. Now, look around this space and see all the gifts that are revealed to you. Know that you have many gifts and talents that are a part of you. When you have savored your gifts, you can go back to the elevator and descend, returning to the earthly level of existence.

Heartstring Meditation

Once again, make sure you sit comfortably in a chair with your back erect, so that the energy can easily flow up and down your spine. Repeat the awareness part of the above exercise by acknowledging your breath and then bringing your mind to each part of your body. Remember that meditation is merely an inward focus. It is not to be forced. Place your awareness on the present moment.

In this exercise, imagine or feel that your heart opens and a tube of exquisite green, divine light emerges out the top of your heart and ascends through your body, out the top of your head, and straight toward heaven. Take a few moments to let it reach its destination—to your all-knowing and wise self. As you focus, you will begin to receive information, guidance, and insight returning from heaven through the tube and into your mind and heart. Observe how pure the thoughts are that are coming back down to you. If you have a question, ask your Higher Self. As you ask, see the question flow up the tube. Wait a few seconds and see the response descend down into your consciousness. A by-product of this exercise is universal healing energy that is coming from heaven into you. Use it. Enjoy the transformation. At the end of the meditation, seal yourself in a white and golden light of love.

You Are What You Think

The Universe always gives you exactly what you persistently think, so pay close attention to your thoughts. For instance, if throughout the day you think about, talk about, and worry about how to pay your bills, you are creating more of the same worrisome thoughts. Get into the habit of changing every anxious thought into a positive one. I like to use "Cancel" or "Clear" to nullify what I have just mistakenly put out into the Universe. You can use words like "Deflect" or "Never mind" or create your own original, fun vocabulary to turn negative thoughts around. Replace them with positive expressions and optimism with every opportunity that presents itself to you.

Change is never easy, but one thing is certain: you can never be the same person you were five years ago, ten years ago, or even one year ago. Change is constant. A friend told me that when he was young, his family was poor, and he slept in the living room on the couch until he was around nine years old. There was a lot of worry and anxiety over money as he was growing up. Recently, he was reminded of his childhood when he saw two farmworkers fixing an old, beat-up truck on the side of the road. He remembers being in a similar situation, always worrying about having enough money to fix his car. "If I hadn't started on my spiritual quest and learned to meditate every day, I would still be in the same jam," he said. But my friend's awareness grew. Because of his inner work, his whole life had changed, and no longer did he have to worry about money, fixing cars, or sleeping on the couch. He is not the same person he once was because he was willing to change.

Each day is a brand-new opportunity to see the world in a different way and to try new things. Like my friend, if we want to make changes and stop clinging to past realities, we can. We begin by taking conscious responsibility for our choices and decisions in life, because what we think today will create our tomorrow. Having this understanding, we can free ourselves from past belief systems and emotional blackmail by others. We can continue to grow, to evolve, and to become more aware. When we look to the future and not the past, we give ourselves permission to receive what is new. We are creating with our imagination unlimited possibilities for our future. We become attuned to the Formless One or Love. Unconditional love, first of self, then of others, will assist us in abandoning the old ways and discovering new ones.

Living life comes down to this. You need to spend less time worrying, making excuses, and procrastinating. No more thinking of things you have not accomplished. Start doing them, or make a new list. What situations in your life do you still need to handle? Do you have a clear idea of what success is or what it means to you? Are you happy financially? Do you like the way you look and feel physically? Are your needs being met emotionally? What do you want out of life?

As you change your perspective, coincidences and synchronicities become part of your life—opportunities start knocking at your door. This is all because you have begun to believe in who you truly are. It is time to dream again. Make the changes necessary to feed your soul.

TWELVE

Finished Business

Finish each day and be done with it. You have done what you could. Some blunders and absurdities no doubt creep in. Forget them as soon as you can. Tomorrow is a new day. You shall begin it well and serenely.

—Ralph Waldo Emerson

My own personal rule of thumb for living is to try to see everything as part of the larger picture that includes both worlds. When I die and return home to the spirit world, will I be proud of the life I have just lived or will I be consumed by regrets and missed opportunities? Being mindful of the long view has certainly guided me to be more aware of the way I choose to live and what I am able to give back to this earth.

In your consciousness right now, you have reached a fork in the road. You can choose to change your perspective and, from this moment on, be in control of your life and the choices you make; you can admit to yourself that you are in complete control and clearly realize the impact you have. Or you can stay stagnant in the comfortable world created from your past and think of yourself as just a victim of your circumstances. Now is the time to choose. The victory of a life well lived is measured purely by the love you have created for yourself and others on the planet. Failures can be seen merely as the opportunities you had to demonstrate love, compassion, and forgiveness to yourself and others, but choose not to follow through on.

Going through life with unfinished business slows down our spiritual progress. Life offers us so many situations, painful and otherwise, that either make us stronger or keep us stuck. I have worked with many parents who have lost children, and because a child's death seems so unnatural, so against the grain of what we know about the scheme of life, they can't fit it into their reality. After all, children are not supposed to die before their parents. That is not the way it is *supposed* to be. I sympathize greatly with them, for this is the toughest loss possible, if there is such a thing. However, looking at the larger picture helps. Perhaps their child's death was a lesson that the family group soul, including the child, had to agree upon and experience in order for them to progress spiritually. Perhaps the death was a catalyst of sorts—helping them to evolve.

I have also worked with untold numbers of people who were unable to forgive and forget. Many others were stuck in regret at not having had the chance to say good-bye to someone. Then there were victims so traumatized by abuse, molestation, and destructive childhoods that their lives were immobilized by fear and resentment. This is not living. This is a lot of unfinished business.

When life deals us pain and hurt, we have to rely on our Higher Self to see us through. When we don't deal with the situation, it becomes an open wound that festers. The hurt becomes even bigger, because we didn't take care of it when it happened. By now, we have blown the situation way out of proportion and made it worse than it ever was originally. If we ever want to move forward, we must express our feelings and resolve any unfinished business. So how do we, once and for all, move on?

First, make use of psychotherapy for handling your deep-seated blocks. I have found from my own experience that therapy affords a safe environment to express thoughts and feelings. Therapists are objective. They don't sit in judgment of your situation and usually have your highest good in mind. You, on the other hand, are too close to a past experience to see it clearly. Therapists are able to see with brand-new eyes that are not clouded by proximity and history.

Another way is to discuss the situation with a close friend you trust or perhaps with a support group. Use an environment that feels safe to you. When you discuss your issues with others, old memories come up, and you are forced to bring the situation into the present. This is very valuable. Not only does it give you additional points of view, but also you have the opportunity to see the circumstance from your current perspective, perhaps articulating the situation in light of knowledge acquired in the interim. Together, those two things may very well lead you to understanding and acceptance.

Another very successful method is writing a letter. If you can't seem to forgive, or if someone has died and you weren't able to say good-bye, express your feelings in a letter to that person. You can choose whether or not to actually mail the letter in the case of a living person. The idea here is to get the emotions out of you and onto paper, thus freeing yourself up so that you have more room for love.

The final technique is journaling. Buy a special journal that you reserve for a particular situation. Find a place, perhaps a park or a beach, where you will not be disturbed. Describe your hurt in written word, including why you are holding on to it and what the hurt is teaching your soul. Finally, ask your Higher Self what you need to do to let it go.

You will never completely get over the death of a loved one or the pain of a divorce or even childhood abuse, but at least you can release pent-up tears and express your hidden feelings. Once you do, you will come out the other end a different, more whole being. I promise you.

Starting to have an honest and loving relationship with yourself is the best thing you can do.

Leonard Cohen, a wonderful singer, songwriter, and poet, once said: "Everything that is beautiful is cracked; that's how the light gets in." I believe these words capture the essence of how living through past hurts, disappointments, broken hearts, anger, and fear can heal us. We all must go through the terrible experiences to perhaps become a little bit more humble, compassionate, understanding, patient, truthful, and, in effect, genuinely human. Each of us is an amalgam of feelings, thoughts, emotions, beliefs, histories, experiences, and so forth. These are the things that define us. When we begin to accept ourselves with all the flaws that are an integral part of our design, we will discover how truly beautiful we are. Our self-acceptance will be radiated as an inner goodness that is evident to all who come into our space.

When we become self-actualized, we come into our power, because we have transcended our imperfections and focused on our strengths. We no longer need to be enslaved by our guilt, by "what if" and "what might have been." Instead, we take what we need from any experience and grow. We move on to a new day filled with new knowledge. That is what Cohen meant by "that's how the light gets in." We become enlightened. So, please go right ahead and shine your light so that others can see, feel, and learn from you. What better teacher than you, a person who has lived through a painful experience, to show an easier way to the next person.

KEYS TO FINISHED BUSINESS

Faith

Many people think of faith as either a feeling or a collection of ideas that represent one's convictions. Although both of these concepts involve elements of faith, the full definition is much broader. "Faith," as translated from the Greek, *pistis,* means "firm persuasion" and "a conviction based upon hearing." Faith is something you believe with your total being. It is a sense of knowing and really giving yourself over to something. Faith comes down to pure trust. I am not referring to "blind faith," but true faith.

It seems that the concept of faith is more difficult to grasp for those of us who tend to be very logical in our thinking. Faith is not a tangible thing that can be scientifically measured, nor is it something that you take a class in. Faith is just something you must allow yourself to feel and to experience. For instance, I have faith in my family, trusting that they only have my best interests at heart. I have faith in my editor and the publisher of this book, knowing that they will do their utmost to make this book the best it can be. I have faith in you, readers, to use this book to take steps toward profound healing and life-changing experiences.

Our faith is constantly being tested. For instance, a woman loses her entire family in a tragedy, or a man is laid off from work after twenty years of service, or someone is beaten senseless in front of onlookers who do nothing to help. Is our faith challenged in these instances? You bet. When we question our faith, we go deep within and find if we have enough belief, enough *faith,* to get through it. Faith is especially necessary not when things seem to be going well, but in times of tragedy. During these times our faith can help us to persevere; it can help us to find a reason to keep on. When things seem their darkest, faith is truly a miracle. Your faith has gotten you this far in life. So, never give up. Keep the faith, especially in yourself.

Clear Conscience

Often when a situation that we had a hand in does not turn out for the best, we find the result difficult to accept. We feel that *if only* we could have done something differently, the outcome would have been better.

We hold on to guilty feelings and beat ourselves up for doing something *wrong*. We find it extremely hard to accept that we were doing the very best we could with the information we had.

Doing the right thing cannot be judged solely by the outcome or by the opinions of others. Making good decisions—doing the right thing—is a constant part of life. Should you take that other job? Do you tell your friend that her husband is having an affair? Should you have an abortion? Do you pull your father off the resuscitator? Do you call the cops about your relative for whom there's an arrest warrant out?

Making the right choice can be difficult enough, and you alone are accountable for the choices you make. But the more time you take to listen to your inner guidance, the more you will be aware of *your* truth—who you are and what you stand for. The more you realize that you have the insights right inside you, the easier it will be to have a clear conscience.

THE FINAL ACT OF LOVE

Several years ago I did a reading in Seattle that has stayed with me. This particular reading had to do with a very difficult choice and about doing the right thing.

A couple were sitting together off on the right side of the room. I could see that they were stressed. However, only when a spirit is present do I actually approach someone. Suddenly, a young male spirit stood behind this couple and revealed to me a hospital room.

I spoke to the audience. "There is a young man here. He has blond hair and blue eyes. He seems to be a very gentle sort of soul. He is in a hospital bed in a coma. Does this . . ."

Before I could finish the sentence, the couple stood up. I walked over to them.

The woman spoke first. "I knew he would be here tonight."

"Do you know this young man?" I asked.

"Yes. He's our son."

The audience murmured.

"He is on some sort of resuscitator. I don't see him moving," I said.

"Yes," the woman replied, as she began to cry. "He was in an accident."

"Now he is showing me the accident. He fell off some scaffolding. Was he on a construction site?"

The man just nodded his head in confirmation. I could tell these two were in a lot of pain. As I tuned into their emotional centers, I could feel the pain they were living within their hearts. The only way to describe it was that I felt as if a huge rock was resting on my chest and I was unable to breathe.

"Is his name Jimmy or Jamie, like mine?"

"Jamie."

"Jamie came here to tell you that he's okay and that you did the right thing. He is very happy and wants to thank you."

At this point I thought the woman was going to collapse. She let out a loud cry. The rest of the audience seemed on the verge of tears as well. The couple hugged one another as I listened to Jamie.

"Jamie loves you very much, and he wants you to know that he feels your love all the time. He is sorry that you had to go through so much pain."

The couple nodded their heads in understanding.

"Who is Chip or Kip?" I asked.

"Chip is our other son. He's still alive," the woman replied.

"Jamie is saying that Chip has to forgive you. He had no right to interfere. You did the right thing."

Just then, I got the entire picture. "You took your son off life support, didn't you?"

"Yes." This time it was the gentleman who spoke.

"Chip fought with you over this. He didn't want you to pull the plug. He called you murderers."

With this comment, the woman began to cry all over again.

"Well, you did a compassionate act for Jamie. He is saying that he didn't want to stay on earth anymore. He wanted to be free to go on. And you helped him."

By now, there were many people in the audience crying along with the couple.

"Jamie is thanking you for releasing his spirit to heaven."

"What about Chip?" the woman asked.

I looked into her eyes. "You did what you did out of love. It will take Chip some time to learn this lesson. Be patient with him. He doesn't see the whole picture. Just keep loving him no matter what."

The woman and man thanked me profusely.

Compassion

Most of us feel that the world would be a better place if everybody would think the way we do. Chip certainly wanted his parents to think and believe as he did about not disconnecting the resuscitator on his brother. Like many of us, he looked at life from his own egocentric point of view. When others don't think the way we do, we tend to be intolerant and not honor them. Compassion opens our hearts to feel another person's pain. It is important to care and to be compassionate, because our awareness of others and the world at large deepens. Compassion reinforces charity, empathy, and sympathy. The heart is the strongest muscle in the human body, and when we exercise it, it grows.

When you begin to exercise compassion, you will inevitably meet those old emotions that are ready to close down your heart, such as judgment, racism, sexism, and so forth. But at the same time, you will begin to understand the relatedness of everyone living on the planet. In order to come into wholeness, you will have to work through past memories and feelings of unkindness and cruelty. These feelings arise out of deep emotional wounds and clearly tell you that you need to have more compassion for yourself. When you show compassion first for yourself, it is much easier to feel compassion toward others.

Gratitude

Compassion and gratitude go hand in hand. When you have compassion, you are grateful for the little things that bring joy to your life. My gratitude routine is simple. I wake up, go downstairs to my living room, and look at the view of the ocean in front of me. Then I take a quick gaze at my garden and the blue skies above me and thank the forces that be for giving me such a beautiful place in which to live— one that makes me feel safe, secure, and happy. Not a day goes by without my being grateful for everything I have.

We have all heard the following expressions, "Be grateful; it could have been worse," and "Be thankful—you still have your health." Gratitude is the feeling we have when we learn that our loved one has survived a deadly crash. It is the feeling we experience upon hearing that our tumor is benign. Being grateful helps us to keep things in perspective, because it is true—things could always be worse. And it is certainly natural to feel thankful after overcoming adversity.

On the other hand, it is okay to feel ungrateful or be angry over a loss you feel you didn't deserve, as long as you understand that you don't have to feel this way forever. Whenever I start to feel ungrateful, I make a list of all the things for which I am grateful. I may not be in the mood to do it, but it does help to pull me out of fear, so I can see things a little more clearly. There is too much in life for which we can be happy and grateful. We don't have to let one thing bring us down or cause us to become angry. There is so much positivism on which to focus. Make a list of things to be grateful for and, when you're down, take it out and reflect on it.

You can also look at the bad things and difficult people and situations in your life and be grateful for the incredible learning opportunities they have afforded you, not to mention the blessings that come from adversity. When you look back at your life, become aware of how the tough times brought you immeasurable growth.

A LIFE WELL LIVED

I find that the members of most families (including extended ones) are truly able to recognize the love and magic they share with each other. They are grateful for being a part of a family and with people they can love and trust. Such was a family I met during a lecture in upstate New York. This next reading also reinforces the idea that it is important to finish what you came on this earth to do.

It was summertime, so the weather was a bit humid. We were assembled in a meeting hall, and I had begun the reading portion of my lecture. I remember a fan blowing in the back of the room because it made a funny noise. There were many people in the audience who seemed to know one another, so, on the one hand, I felt a little uncomfortable but, on the other, I also felt very cozy.

I began with my prayer and brief commentary about the way I work and how spirits speak to me. Suddenly a gentleman dressed in a suit and tie began pointing to a part of the hall. I moved toward the spirit and listened to what he had to say.

I could hear the spirit say, *Tell them that I am so happy. They don't have to cry over me anymore.* I asked the spirit for further information as identification. He showed me a cabin in the woods. It was a charming place—very rustic. It looked like a dollhouse.

I explained to the audience, "There is a distinguished-looking man standing here pointing to a cabin in the woods. Does anyone recognize this?"

Two middle-aged women in the front of the room raised their hands.

"Do you know the name Fred or maybe Ted?" I asked.

"Teddy!" they screeched in unison.

I smiled, then listened for some more information.

"Teddy. Is he your father? He is saying, *My girls.*"

"Yes! That's him."

"He is telling me that he forgives you both. Did you take his car? Because he is showing me a tan convertible and two young girls in it."

One of the women spoke. "Yes, we went for a joyride in his new car many years ago."

"He is saying that he loved that car and was so mad at the both of you, but he forgives you."

"We're sorry, Pop," said the other daughter.

"What are your names?" I asked.

"I'm Hanna and she's Abby."

"Do you have another sibling? I see a young boy with your father."

"Yes. Our brother Chris, but he's not dead."

"No. He's saying this is someone else. Did your father have a younger brother?"

"Uncle Roy."

"Teddy is saying that he was so happy to make up with his brother. He is saying that he learned his lesson."

"They had a big fight and didn't talk to each other for, I don't know, maybe ten years."

"Your father is glad they made up before he died. He is saying that he is very proud of all of you."

"He was the best. We miss you, Pop," Abby uttered.

"Now he is showing me the cabin again. There is a group of people standing outside under a live oak tree. He is saying thank you for having his memorial service at the old cabin."

"We knew he would like it there. It was his favorite place in the whole world."

"He lives in a cabin just like it in heaven. He says that he is at peace."

The two women became teary-eyed.

"Your father was a very gentle man. He is saying that he got everything out of life he wanted. He is guiding the next generation."

"He loved being a grandfather. He had seven grandchildren."

"He will be watching over all of you."

Teddy was at peace, because he lived his life the way he wanted and left earth with a clear conscience.

A Positive Attitude

To attract positive, joyful, and prosperous situations to you, you must be that way yourself. If you have an open, loving, positive attitude, anything burdensome in life can be lightened. Therefore, it is important to be aware of your mood. It is created by your thoughts. Good thoughts create a good mood. Negative thoughts create a bad mood. Your mood and attitude affect everyone with whom you come in contact. Attitude drives behavior. A particular attitude, like a particular kind of clothing, is what other people see. Every day you have a choice of how you will behave, the mood you will give out to the world, and how you want people to know you.

Your attitude permeates the space around you. If you feel angry, you can choose to go through your day with an angry attitude, but be aware of its effect. All who engage with you will take a part of that anger with them. Is that what you want to give out to the world? Staying angry won't necessarily make you feel better, and it will probably make you feel worse.

I am not saying to never be angry. It's important not to bury or deny emotions, so that you know what you are truly feeling. Just keep the bigger picture in mind as you determine what to *do* with your feelings. You always have two choices. One is to be in control of your feelings and behavior. The other is to have your emotions control you.

Finally, isn't it about time that you let go of your ego-based hurts? Isn't it about time you call that family member or friend and say "I'm sorry" for whatever happened between the two of you? Forgive yourself and the other person. It doesn't take much to pick up that phone or write that e-mail and demonstrate love. If you have to take the high road and admit that perhaps you were wrong, now is the time. Don't put off till tomorrow what you can do today, for there is a chance you may not see tomorrow.

Hope

Hope, like faith, is something intangible that cannot be measured. Hope is not wishful thinking, but a very essential ingredient of life. In fact, I don't think anyone could effectively sustain life without it. It is a natural part of our makeup. The element of hope keeps us dreaming, creating, and overcoming obstacles. It is that unseen spark that motivates many of us to live a full and productive life. It is a deep-down personal belief that there will be a positive outcome. Even the worst of circumstances can be overcome with a sense of hope for a better tomorrow. Hope is from the heart. It awakens us to our own truth and helps to form our unique spirituality.

We must remember that each day is completely different from the next. Obstacles of the past, whether self-imposed or formed by others, may cling to us, yet inside of us resides the solution for change. Our life has a meaning. Tomorrow will not be the same as today. Even if we think it will be the same, there is always something to make it different, because each day is filled with the magic of hope and possibilities. We can discover a new aspect of ourselves and others that we never knew existed.

FAMILY REUNION

People often ask, "James, what do you get out of doing this work?" As you read this next story, you will completely understand. Several years ago I had the opportunity to bring through messages to a family who had traveled over twelve hundred miles to see me. I had just finished my meditation portion of the event when I began to sense a very strong smell of smoke. I looked over at my right side and became aware of the spirit of a golden retriever licking my right hand. Standing next to the dog was the spirit of a young boy about nine years old wearing a Little League uniform and a red hat. He said to me, *I want to talk to my dad.* He pointed to a man sitting at the end of the third row to my right. I looked at a middle-aged, oversized man sitting in the chair. Two young girls about seventeen and fifteen were sitting directly to his left. As the spirit boy pointed in that direction, the dog sauntered over to the girls and circled around them.

"Sir," I said, "there is a young man here about nine years old who says he is your son. He is accompanied by a golden retriever."

The light-haired girl put her hands up to her mouth and screamed, "Oh my God!"

The man instantly began to cry, shaking his head that he understood what I was relaying.

I continued, "He says his name is Paulie, and he is here with another, older boy named Kenny."

This caused a huge reaction from both girls and their father. They immediately began to hug one another.

"Those are our brothers!"

At this point, several audience members came over to the man and his daughters in support. The shaken man sat back down. As I pierced through his emotion, I became aware of a spirit woman standing behind him and patting his hair. *I told you I would never leave you!* she mouthed. I mentally asked her what her name was. She replied, *Rose.*

"Now there is a woman standing behind you, sir, who says her name is Rose."

The man looked down and then shook his head yes. One of the girls screamed, "That's our mother."

"She promised me she would never leave me! I was hoping she wouldn't," the father said.

"And she hasn't," I chimed in. "She's right behind you."

Then all of a sudden the three spirits caught the excitement of piercing the veil between worlds and started throwing thoughts at me all at once. I began to spit them out as fast as I could.

"They have seen Nana Jean. Grandpa was also there to greet them. Paulie says that he is playing baseball over there, and Kenny still brings Lucky for walks."

Then the mother, Rose, calmed the boys down. Still standing behind her husband, she transferred thoughts and images to my head.

I looked over at the two girls, and said, "Your mother wants me to tell you that she wants you to please contact Mr. Johnson's family and convey a message to them. She wants them to know that he died nobly—attempting to save another life. There is no greater achievement in life than that."

The family acknowledged this comment. Immediately, I could smell smoke.

"Did your family die in a fire?"

"Yes, they did," said the father.

"Kenny is screaming at me, *But we are alive! We didn't really die!*"

I looked over at the father again, and he was crying while at the same time saying, "Thank you. This was my last hope—that my family lived on. You have no idea how much you have given us."

I then noticed that the dog was licking the girls' hands and told them so.

Both girls bowed their heads in tears, as the older one replied, "That makes sense. He saved us. Lucky woke us up in the middle of the night and got us out of the house. Our mom ran back in for the boys, but didn't make it out."

With that, the mother had a message for her daughters. "Your mother is saying that you have not been left behind for nothing. You each have a lot to accomplish, especially helping others. You must learn from this to assist others through life and death and know that your mother and brothers are right behind you cheering you on. They will help you from their side of life."

Then Rose screamed into my ear, and I turned to her husband and said, "Rose says, *You got it wrong. We are not in the ground. We are more alive than you!*" Then I saw her laugh.

"That's Rosie. That's her sense of humor, all right. Thank you, Mr. Van Praagh. You have done something incredible. You have given our family back to us. You have given us hope. Now we know we are never alone, and we are still together. We will be with them always. Thank you."

And with that comment, Lucky barked!

We all share a common bond, whether we are part of a family or have a family of friends. Each one of us wants to find our purpose, live our truth, and express ourselves without judgment or bias. With this desire comes a desire for freedom. When you are true to yourself and live each day in truth, you will find your freedom.

You have chosen to come back at this time and place to achieve greatness in life and peace in your soul. Your hope is that life has meaning and that you are worthwhile. Let this moment be a turning point in your life. You are reading this book to see yourself in a new light and accept the greatness that is you. Begin now by cleaning up the unfinished business of your past that keeps you from being self-realized and whole. With your newfound freedom, "should've," "would've," and "could've" will be no more.

MY LOVING FRIEND

A few days after that very profound dream in which I saw my friend Violette, I couldn't stop thinking about it, and I began to reminisce about the time we first met. It was about ten years ago, when I moved into my current home in California. One morning, I was in front of my house picking up the morning paper when a man in a meat truck stopped and inquired if I was James.

I said, "Yes."

He went on to say that the woman at the end of the street had mentioned that I had just moved in.

"What's her name?" I asked.

"Violette," he continued. "She really wants to meet you. She's seen you on television." Then the man in the meat truck waved good-bye and drove down the street.

I remember thinking to myself that I was sure she was nice, but I felt leery about introducing myself. I knew that we would eventually meet each other.

During the months that followed, I met several of the neighbors on my block. Each one asked the same question, "Have you met Violette yet?"

I couldn't help but wonder who this Violette was and what was so special about her that was making everyone push me to meet her.

The following week my curiosity got the better of me. I pulled out my first book, *Talking to Heaven*, and walked down the street to meet the mysterious Violette.

When I reached her house, I walked down brown-painted wooden stairs and noticed a variety of footwear sitting outside the bright red front door. Little did I know that this was a metaphor for what was waiting for me.

I knocked on the door and heard a deep, raspy-sounding voice, one that could only be acquired after years of cigarettes and whiskey, say, "Who is it?"

The door opened, and a petite woman with great big green eyes and a huge smile said, "Oh my God, James Van Praagh."

I immediately felt an incredible rush of energy go through my body as if I were reconnecting with an old soul with whom I had shared many lifetimes. It felt familiar and at the same time a bit peculiar.

"I've been waiting for you," she said. "Would you like a cup of tea?"

She pulled a newspaper off of the couch, and I sat down, mesmerized by my surroundings.

"Sure. Thank you."

Violette went into the kitchen and kept on repeating, "Oh my, I can't believe it!"

As I sat on the couch, I looked at the beautiful collection of antique statuary and glassware lining the room. The walls were covered with incredible California impressionist paintings of hillsides and flowers, one more beautiful than the next.

I called out, "I love your paintings. Are you a collector?"

Violette walked back in the room with a tray of cups. "Those are all local artists. You know, I go junking every weekend," she said as she placed a cup in front of me.

"Junking?"

"Yes. Yard sales, garage sales. Somebody's garbage can be your treasure, and you can find some good deals!" Violette had a glint in her eye.

"Yes, I've heard that before."

She then went on to tell me that she had seen me on television. She looked directly at me and said as she was sipping her tea, "I believe like you. We've got to stick together. People have to know the truth. Oh, isn't God wonderful?"

I knew she meant it rhetorically.

Violette shared her experience in the "program"—Alcoholics Anonymous—for thirty years. "It taught me how to appreciate God in everything and everyone." She paused for a moment. "Isn't it a shame, James, that people don't believe in themselves? They can't see the power they have. You know people don't realize that they create their world with their thoughts and how they treat one another."

I was stunned at Violette's observations. I knew instantly why the rest of the neighborhood had wanted me to meet her. They all probably knew that we two were obviously cut from the same cloth.

"Have you finished your tea yet?" she asked.

"Yes, I have."

"Give it here," she said reaching over for it.

I wasn't sure what she was going to do with it, but I handed it to her.

She turned the cup over, dumping most of the tea leaves onto the saucer. "This is Turkish tea."

Violette began to survey the remnants left on the bottom of the cup. "Oh, I see you will be writing two books . . . Oh, and look here, you are going to have a show on television about ghosts." She looked at me and smiled. "But they won't do it right."

She then looked back down and said, "Your health is good, and you help many people."

I thanked her.

"Okay, now you can leave. Come back whenever you want."

And so began one of the most incredible and loving spiritual connections I have shared with anyone in my life. We used to call each other every day to make sure everything was okay. She once told me she had a "significant other" and they were living "in sin." I remember the time she had come to a party at my house wearing a straitjacket as a joke, which my dinner guests overwhelmingly enjoyed.

Violette was indeed a character. I could not help but love her. Besides being the local neighborhood gossip, she had a way of knowing everything that happened within a two-mile radius. I believe that she was really the neighborhood "seer."

We spent hours philosophizing about life, death, and the great beyond. She would often ask, "How come the people of the world don't recognize the opportunities to demonstrate kindness?"

Our deep, loving friendship lasted for ten years until that fateful day when I got a phone call from a nervous Violette.

"James, they found a massive blockage in my heart and want to operate." The next week, Violette was in the ICU, and I went to visit her the night before her procedure.

The moment I walked into her room, I felt an overwhelming sadness. Lying there was a force to be reckoned with who was at the end of her days.

As I talked to her, I became aware of several spirits standing behind her, anticipating her arrival.

"There's a man named Bill who wants to let you know he is here."

"That is my husband. God bless him."

Those were among her final words. Violette never made it out of the hospital. She suffered a stroke on the operating table. The only other time I would see Bill's face was when he appeared in my dream several months later as the mystery man.

Now, of course, I realize that the dream I had been having all along was about Violette sharing her death scene with me.

A few days after I had figured out my dream, I was watering the plants in my garden. Suddenly I looked up, and standing next to the bird of paradise was a radiant Violette surrounded by an otherworldly light.

"Thank you, James," she said. "I am sorry for confusing you in the dream, but I never got a chance to say thank you for being my friend these past years. I want you to know that we all get our rewards, whether we are givers of love or receivers of love. We are never alone when we feel another's love. I needed to let you know that in order to make sure I left no unfinished business behind."

In memoriam
Violette McKevitt
May 26, 2008

BIBLIOGRAPHY

Ashton, Robert. *The Life Guide: Ten Things You Need to Know About Everything That Matters.* Upper Saddle River, NJ: FT Press, 2008.

Bays, Brandon. *The Journey: A Practical Guide to Healing Your Life and Setting Yourself Free.* New York: Simon & Schuster, Fireside, 1999.

Beazley, Hamilton. *No Regrets: A Ten-Step Program for Living in the Present and Leaving the Past Behind.* Hoboken, NJ: Wiley, 2004.

Cayce, Edgar. *Soul and Spirit: Fully Understand Yourself and Your Life.* Virginia Beach, VA: A.R.E. Press, 2006.

Coleman, Paul. *Life's Parachutes: How to Land on Your Feet During Trying Times.* New York: Dell, 1993.

Dalai Lama, His Holiness the. *Live in a Better Way: Reflections on Truth, Love, and Happiness.* New York: Penguin Compass, 2001.

Dowrick, Stephanie. *Choosing Happiness: Life and Soul Essentials.* New York: Tarcher, Penguin, 2005.

Erikson, Erik H. *The Life Cycle Completed.* New York: Norton, 1998.

Finley, Guy. *The Secret of Letting Go.* Woodbury, MN: Llewellyn, 2007.

Goldsmith, Joel S. *Awakening Mystical Consciousness.* Atlanta: Acropolis, 1980.

Hallowell, Edward M. *Dare to Forgive.* Deerfield Beach, FL: Health Communications, 2004.

Hammer, Frank L. *Life and Its Mysteries.* Philadelphia: Dorrance, 1945.

Hill, Dawn. *Reaching for the Other Side.* North Hollywood, CA: Newcastle, 1983.

Joy, W. Brugh. *Joy's Way: A Map for the Transformational Journey: An Introduction to the Potentials for Healing with the Body Energies.* Los Angeles: Tarcher, 1979.

Mack, Joshua. *Karma 101: What Goes Around Comes Around . . . And What You Can Do About It.* Gloucester, MA: Fair Winds Press, 2002.

Michie, David. *Buddhism for Busy People: Finding Happiness in an Uncertain World.* Crows Nest, Australia: Allen & Unwin, Inspired Living, 2007.

Roman, Sanaya. *Spiritual Growth: Being Your Higher Self.* Tiburon, CA: Kramer, 1989.

Smedes, Lewis B. *Forgive and Forget: Healing the Hurts We Don't Deserve.* New York: HarperCollins, 1984.

Sugrue, Thomas. *There Is a River: The Story of Edgar Cayce.* Virginia Beach, VA: A.R.E. Press, by arrangement with Holt, Rinehart and Winston, 1942.

Tavris, Carol, and Elliot Aronson. *Mistakes Were Made (But Not by Me): Why We Justify Foolish Beliefs, Bad Decisions, and Hurtful Acts.* Orlando, FL: Harcourt, 2007.

Thondup, Tulku. *Boundless Healing: Meditation Exercises to Enlighten the Mind and Heal the Body.* Boston and London: Shambhala, 2000.

White Eagle. *Awakening: A Guide for Living with Death and Dying.* Hampshire, UK: White Eagle Publishing Trust, 2002.

Yogananda, Paramahanda. *Man's Eternal Quest.* Los Angeles: Self-Realization Fellowship, 1975.

ACKNOWLEDGMENTS

Brian Preston—Thank you for always taking my hand and guiding me to the high road.

Maura Fortune—Life's wonderful moments are much more special when they are shared with a sister like you. Thank you for so freely giving your laughter and love.

The Barry family—May Irish eyes always smile upon you.

Joerdie Fisher—You truly are the Divine Mother ... because that's how you roll.

Mary Ann Saxon—Merci beaucoup for your belief and encouragement. You are truly my soul mate, n'est-ce pas?

Kelley Dennis—If laughter is the best medicine, then you are my favorite doctor.

Jeffrey Eisenberg—Your friendship is among the oldest one I have, and that is amazing considering how young I am.

Chip McAllister—Hearing your voice always brightens my day! Thanks for keeping life continuously interesting and full of surprises!

Ken Robb—The yang to my yin. There is no one else I would rather share a birthday with than my evil twin. The "fatherland" will always be ours.

Marion McGarry—From the moment I met you I knew we had known each other for eons of time. Thank you for your support, friendship, and above all the laughs. My stomach still aches!

Christian Dickens—Your performances are legendary! I am forever grateful to be part of your three-ring circus.

Cyndi Schacher—Thank you for your sparkling point of view of the world and those who inhabit her. There is no one else whom I would rather carpool with.

Joe Skeehan—You have a true heart. Thank you for always keeping an eye on my earthly matters while my head is in the clouds.

Marilyn Jensen—Follow the path of the star. You have enriched many. Thank you for illuminating us all with your brilliant light over these many years.

Jacquie Ochoa—Thank you for all of the TLC. Your inquisitive perspective of the world always keeps us on our toes. Your kindness is only matched by your intelligence.

Scott E. Schwimer—Blessings for all you are in my life. Thank you for always lending an ear and sharing a Web site when I need it most.

Tori Mitchell—Your sweet and selfless disposition is always welcome in my house, along with your deviled eggs and black olives.

Randy Wilson—My go-to guy for all things desert, cars, and design. Your friendship is appreciated as much as it is dependable.

Dorothea Delgado—Sistah D! Your insight into the world we live in astounds even me.

Kelley Kreinbrink—I am so appreciative for all you have done on my behalf over these several years. I hope the world seems sweeter to you now that you have been touched by Spirit.

Cammy Farone—My immeasurable gratitude and appreciation for the many years of your selfless dedication. Thank you for gifting me with not only your artistic talent, but also the demonstration of your compassion to others.

HarperOne—A thank you to each and every one of you for so kindly giving me a platform to enlighten the millions who feel so lost. I am grateful to be part of your family and appreciate your making me feel so much at home.

Gideon Weil—I must have done something right in my past life to have an editor as good as you in this present one.

Suzanne Wickham—Thank you for your incredible organizational ability, professionalism, and hard work in assuring the world knows who I am.

Andrew Lear–Let's put on a show! Thank you for navigating me through the rapids of Hollywood and steering me clear of the body snatchers.

Jan Miller–Thank you for the inspiration behind this book; and to everyone at Dupree Miller who assisted me in bringing its words to the world.